3 9082 09408 0796

FAST TRACK ADOPTION

D0104503

AUBURN HILLS PUBLIC LIBRARY
3400 E. Seyburn Drive
AUBURN HILLS, MI 48326

Susan Burns, Psy.D.

FAST TRACK
ADOPTION

*The Faster,
Safer Way to Privately
Adopt a Baby*

ST. MARTIN'S GRIFFIN ☙ NEW YORK

AUBURN HILLS PUBLIC LIBRARY
3400 E. Seyburn Drive
AUBURN HILLS, MI 48326

FAST TRACK ADOPTION.

Copyright © 2003 by Susan Burns, Psy.D.

Foreword © 2003 Karen R. Lane, Esq.

All rights reserved.

Printed in the United States of America.

No part of this book may be used or reproduced in any manner whatsoever without written permission except in the case of brief quotations embodied in critical articles or reviews.

For information, address St. Martin's Press, 175 Fifth Avenue, New York, N.Y. 10010.

www.stmartins.com

Library of Congress Cataloging-in-Publication Data

Burns, Susan
　　Fast track adoption : the faster, safer way to privately adopt a baby / Susan L. Burns.
　　　　p.　cm.
　　Includes bibliographical references (page 257).
　　ISBN 0-312-30701-2
　　1. Adoption.　　I. Title

HV875.B87 2003
362.73'4—dc21   2003047157

First Edition: December 2003

1　3　5　7　9　10　8　6　4　2

To my husband, Scott,

for sharing the journey

To my parents, Jim and Dossie,

for their encouragement and support

To my children, Andy and Malia,

the highlights of my life

3 9082 09408 0796

CONTENTS

FOREWORD

I have been practicing law in the field of adoptions since 1970. While many laws, policies, and philosophies have changed, one aspect has always remained the same—the belief of most hopeful parents that there are no babies to adopt and that their deep desire to adopt a child will remain unfulfilled. Unfortunately, many prospective adopters begin their search with this self-defeating attitude. And as the journey unfolds they tend to invent additional reasons why their hopes will be crushed. For example, they may insist that birth parents possess qualifications and characteristics that are simply impossible to find in the real world. Or they may believe there are few opportunities to meet prospective birth parents. Once a potential birth parent is found, many adoption clients are convinced they will be rejected.

The irony is that by endorsing such beliefs prospective adopters often unwittingly set themselves up for failure, ultimately sabotaging the very dream they profess to hold most dear. Although many hopeful parents have experienced failure along the road to infertility, their fears and negative expectations can create real handicaps when their hopes turn toward adoption. Adoption clients commonly build up their defenses and retreat, much like a turtle in its shell. Rather than embracing the adoption process, those seeking to adopt are often afraid to be proactive. It is much like someone who wants to be married, but doesn't want to go out on a blind date because it might not work out. In adoption, however, as with other important goals in life, one's ability to achieve success is usually enhanced by maintaining a positive attitude, doing the necessary homework, and staying personally engaged throughout the process.

In *Fast Track Adoption*, Susan Burns clears the way for a successful adoption by challenging negative attitudes and preparing readers to begin their search on a more realistic and productive level. Readers are empowered with the practical tools and resources they need to take control of the process and achieve a satisfactory adoption for everyone concerned. When matched with a birth parent, a very warm relationship develops, culminating in the emotional and caring transfer of the baby from the birth parents to the adoptive parents. This book helps prospective parents recognize what they can and must do to achieve a successful match, as well as what they should be looking for to avoid problems that can be catastrophic, both emotionally and financially.

I applaud Susan Burns for her detailed and meticulous guide and I share with her the belief that anyone who dreams of a baby to adopt has the inherent ability to make that dream come true.

Karen R. Lane, Esq.

Karen R. Lane is an attorney practicing adoption law in Santa Monica, California. She is the founder and past president of the American Academy of Adoption Attorneys. Mrs. Lane has represented over four thousand families who have successfully adopted. She is also the proud mother of an adopted daughter.

ACKNOWLEDGMENTS

I have been very fortunate to receive the kind assistance of many people in the writing of this book. I am grateful to my editor, Heather Jackson, for her sharp eye and original suggestions. Karen Lane has been extremely generous in sharing her time, experience, and insights. For reading the book in various stages and providing their advice and encouragement, I would like to thank Judith Sperling-Newton, Mary Lib Mooney, Randy Strong, and Jana Wolff. Special thanks also go the many adoptive families who contributed their personal stories for inclusion in this book. I am particularly indebted to Elsa Hurley, my literary agent, for her enormous support and assistance throughout every phase of this book's development—and to the Maui Writers Conference for providing valuable resources as well as the means by which I met Elsa. I will always be grateful to my family for their steady patience, help, and encouragement during the process of writing this book. I would also like to thank Laurie Loomis, Inez Whitlow, and all of the other many dedicated adoption professionals who worked so hard to make our adoption dreams come true.

NOTE TO THE READER

The author has made every effort to ensure that the information contained in this book is accurate and up-to-date. However, each adoption situation is unique and adoption information often changes. This book cannot address all the issues with which you may be faced. As such, readers of this book may experience various degrees of overall success. The author disclaims any liability for injury suffered due to the information or methods presented herein. In addition, while this book discusses many legal matters, it does not intend to offer legal advice and should not be used as a substitute for obtaining qualified legal counsel. Adoption laws and procedures frequently change and can be interpreted differently within different jurisdictions. Those people considering adoption should retain an attorney before starting their adoption plans.

All personal stories and anecdotes used as examples throughout this book are true. The people cited are real, but their names and identifying information have been changed. The one exception is the sample home study provided in the appendix. The names and information contained in the sample home study have no relation to actual individuals and this information is provided simply as an example of what one might expect in a typical home study report.

FAST TRACK ADOPTION

INTRODUCTION

OUR ADOPTION JOURNEY

In January of 1996, my husband and I decided to pursue adoption to create the family we had been dreaming of for years. We knew nothing about how to adopt, and had no idea where to begin. We neither knew anyone personally who had adopted, nor did we know anyone in the adoption field who could help us. We had heard that it was difficult to adopt. Nevertheless, we were optimistic. After all, we were mature, successful, and determined. And we were confident in our ability to do the necessary research and to clear the required hurdles to complete a successful adoption. Now, I have to laugh at our blissful ignorance. We knew very little then about just how many twists and turns our adoption quest would ultimately take.

Our first setback came shortly after receiving our copy of the *Adoption Guide* listing adoption agencies and their requirements (information on this and other resources appear in the appendix). We had decided to pursue the adoption of a newborn within the United States because as newcomers to the parenting scene, we looked forward to caring for a child right from his or her earliest beginnings. In addition, we wished to receive as much information as possible about our birth parents' medical and social backgrounds. Knowing little about how to proceed, we assumed that agency adoption was the way to go. It was simply what we had always heard. Unfortunately, almost immediately, we learned that we did not meet the eligibility requirements for most domestic adoption agencies. This was despite the fact that we were committed to giving a child our love and every opportunity we could for the most promising life possible, we were financially stable, and we had the full support and enthusiasm of both our extended families. We owned a small farm on Maui with lots of space for safe, healthy out-of-doors play. We are both well educated and have worked with children professionally. Most of the agencies I spoke with took little interest in my doctorate in psychology, the fact that I was licensed in two states, or that I had devoted years to helping children and families in my private practice. Instead, we were disqualified for being too old (I was forty, my husband was forty-three) and for being married less than one year (we were together for four years prior to being married). The final nail in the coffin was the fact that we were not regular churchgoers.

Undeterred, we continued to do our research, convinced that there had to be a few good agencies that would at least consider us as applicants. Finally, after weeks of correspondence and study, we were able to identify a small handful that were willing to work with us. More phone calls, questions, telephone interviews, and reference checks ensued before we finally decided to proceed with an agency in Florida. (They had agreed to waive the length of marriage requirement in our case.) Our decision to choose them was based on the number of infants they placed per year, recommendations of other clients, and the apparent expertise and personal attention we sensed from the staff.

We received the agency's application materials with mixed feelings. In addition to the fee of several thousand dollars, the application itself was lengthy and required us to complete and notarize many different forms. There were forms for prior convictions, traffic offenses, and a clearance from Child Protective Services. In addition, we were required to take child-rearing classes, and to obtain certified training in infant and child first aid and CPR. We also had to create our "autobiographical profile," a written description of ourselves, our home, and why we wished to adopt. I recall feeling dismayed not so much by the amount of work we needed to do but by the length of time it would take us to assemble all the necessary elements to simply become eligible. On the other hand, it was nice to know that we had something concrete to do that, once completed, would advance us on our road to success.

Or so I thought.

Three months later, we sent off our completed application packet along with our payment. We promptly received a letter back from the agency congratulating us for having met all the requirements of the application process. That was the last we ever heard from them. At the time, I was blissfully unaware that anything was wrong. For months, we simply assumed that our profile was being shown to birth mothers and that the perfect match was right around the corner. Periodically, we would call the agency for progress reports, hopeful that we would finally hear some good news. Each time, it was the same story; the person we had spoken with previously was no longer there. No one seemed to know, or to care, who we were. From the time that we received our congratulatory letter, the only further contact we ever got from them was frequent letters soliciting donations. We're still getting them.

Fortunately, several months after completing our application with the agency, we learned that, for a minimal charge, we could apply with an adoption attorney on Oahu. She could put us in touch with pregnant women, and did not have any eligibility requirements. We were elated. We promptly completed the brief application form and submitted this along with our profile.

Again, we waited. In May 1997, almost a year and a half after applying with our attorney, we finally heard some exciting news. She had located a birth mother for us, one that came very close to meeting all of our expectations. The young lady was in New Mexico and was due in early August. She was in need of some living expenses but had her own medical insurance. We obtained medical records as well as photos of her, her husband, and their three children. We also spoke on the phone with both parents on two occasions. Unfortunately, as the delivery time approached, we began to sense trouble. The couple began to break off communication with everyone involved in the adoption plan. They appeared to be screening their calls and could not be contacted by phone. Finally, on the day the baby was to be born, an attorney in New Mexico located the young woman. She was in a different hospital than the one she had identified to us. She had changed her mind.

As heartbreaking as this was, we decided to persevere. Two months later, a birth mother was found by another of our attorney's colleagues, a California attorney named Karen Lane. This time things were different. Karen had a philosophy of open communication between both sets of parents, particularly prior to the child's birth. And we were armed with a new appreciation for speaking directly with our prospective birth parents. With Karen's support and encouragement, we resolved to seek our opportunities to create that personal connection. We had frequent direct contact with our new birth parents. Numerous letters and phone calls were exchanged. As a result, we were much better able to monitor developments and gauge the couple's level of commitment to the adoption plan. Our confidence in this second adoption attempt grew. Likewise, the exchange of information helped the birth parents learn more about us and seemed to strengthen their own confidence in the adoption plan as well. Our beautiful baby boy, Andrew James, was born on October 3, 1997, in Santa Monica, California. The birth parents gave their blessing and their written consent two days later. Three days after that, we flew home as a new family. Our son quickly became the highlight of our lives. In all, it had taken us nearly two years to successfully complete our first adoption.

In January 1999, my husband and I decided to try again. We felt that since we had been down this road before, we would have an easier time the second time around. But this, too, was not to be.

We reapplied with our Hawaii attorney. After waiting for a year and a half, we were finally told of a pregnant woman in Sacramento. She was unmarried and separated from the father. She was due in July. This adoption scenario met all of our hopes except one: the father had not been notified, and therefore his consent was not yet obtained. However, the birth mother told us many times that she, herself, was overwhelmingly in favor of the adoption and that, once notified, the father would not object to the plan. Our attorney explained that as long as the father did not object, the adoption could be successfully completed. However, she did warn us that this situation was considered legally "risky." The decision to proceed was a difficult one. We had been offered a handful of other scenarios in the long months of waiting, but this situation came the closest to matching our expectations. If we turned this one down, how long would it be before we got another chance? The thought of waiting another year and a half seemed unbearable.

So with reservations, we decided to commit. However, it was a decision we were to regret.

After the birth of the baby, we all returned home to Maui with our new daughter. Shortly after this, the birth father surfaced, hired an attorney, and began to aggressively pursue his rights to parent the child. The woman renewed her relationship with the father and changed her mind about the adoption. Because she would not assist us as a witness at the hearing, our chances to complete the adoption were poor. And with both parents no longer in favor of the adoption, my husband and I felt that, ethically, we could not proceed. After living with us for one month, the baby girl we had grown to love was returned to her mother.

Needless to say, we were devastated. Not only was it heartbreaking for us, but it was very difficult for many other members of the family as well. Fortunately our young son Andy rebounded more quickly than the rest of us. I spent many long hours wondering where we went wrong and what we could to do to prevent another disaster like this one. My conclusions drastically altered my impressions of domestic adoption—and led us to another successful adoption, and ultimately to this book.

In January 2001, as we began to put our lives back together after the heartbreak of the previous summer, we embarked on our fourth adoption attempt. This time, in addition to our usual dogged determination, we were armed with an entirely new strategy—one that would leave little to chance. Our goal was to increase our chances for a safe, successful adoption while decreasing the amount of time it required. Our solution was simple. We would become considerably more involved in the initial planning stages of our adoption. Instead of enduring a long, stressful wait while others searched for a birth mother, we now resolved to take the lead ourselves. In short, we were going to use adoption advertising to select our own birth mother. In the process, we hoped to find not just any birth mother, but one who was the right match for us. Once we found her, we planned to maintain frequent contact with her to address her developing needs and to monitor her commitment to the adoption.

On April 19 our birth mother called to say she was in the hospital and our beautiful baby girl, Malia Nicole, was born. All subsequent adoption arrangements proceeded smoothly. Homecoming day was just over three months from the implementation of our new, proactive plan.

Our experiences provided several important lessons. One, while it is important to find a birth mother, it is far more important to find a suitable birth mother—particularly one that has the courage and the commitment to follow through with the adoption plan. Two, it is unnecessary to wait years to find the right birth mother. Adopting parents *do* have other options. There is no hard and fast rule that says you must get in line and wait. Three, although adoption advertising must be done with proper guidance and with certain precautions in mind, getting personally involved and advertising to locate a birth mother is relatively simple and easy to do. While orchestrating an adoption may *sound* like a great deal of work, it really wasn't, since so much of the nonadvertising work was delegated to our adoption professional. *Fast Track Adoption* opens the door to direct communication between both sets of prospective parents prior to making a commitment to proceed. As a result, would-be parents have the opportunity to personally assess the suitability of a proposed match, which can ultimately result in a much safer adoption. Like us, many hopeful adoptive parents may find that getting personally involved in the adoption process is far more preferable than enduring the stress of waiting—or worse, believing your only hope is to take your chances on a potentially risky adoption situation.

Considering its relative ease and effectiveness, it is surprising how little is actually written about using adoption advertising to hasten the domestic adoption process. As a result, most people have no idea how to proceed. This means that they may be vulnerable to unscrupulous or inexperienced adoption arrangers. Or, like us, they may be essentially left to their own devices to discover the best strategy—usually by trial and error and sometimes with disastrous results. Therefore, this book offers a safer and effective alternative to the difficult waiting period that so many prospective parents dread.

Unfortunately, the world of adoption can be overwhelming and confusing, particularly for those new to the scene. The fact that many options exist makes it possible for adopting parents to identify the one method that best suits their own personal style and preferences, and as a result, have a better chance of finding "the best fit." But those seeking to adopt a baby within the United States must sift through seemingly endless volumes of information in order to distill basic relevant information before proceeding. This book does that work for you. It offers readers the safest and fastest possible way to proceed, from the very beginning stages to the final successful completion of a domestic infant adoption.

Adoption, like other seemingly overwhelming tasks, is considerably more manageable when broken down into a series of smaller steps. The Fast Track Adoption process is comprised of a series of easy, but effective, steps:

> #1—Get Ready
> #2—Establish Your Budget
> #3—Assemble Your Professional Team
> #4—Obtain an Approved Home Study
> #5—Prepare an Effective Profile
> #6—Advertise
> #7—Field Calls with Confidence
> #8—Create a Successful Adoption Plan
> #9—Prepare for Your Baby's Homecoming

You need only to complete each step in the proper order to maximize your chances for a safe, efficient domestic infant adoption. Consider this book your adoption "cheat sheet." We've significantly reduced the amount of time you'll spend doing "homework," so that you will more quickly graduate to the joy of becoming adoptive parents.

1

THE FAST TRACK
APPROACH

Having a family is one of life's greatest joys. But millions of men and women are, at some point, faced with an unpleasant personal truth—that the path to parenthood may be one of their biggest challenges. Infertility currently affects at least six million women in this country. Many of these women at some point consider the option of adopting. But to the uninitiated, the world of adoption can seem like a scary place—full of unexpected setbacks, pitfalls, and heartbreaking failures. The very idea of embarking on a difficult and lengthy adoption process can be discouraging to prospective parents, many of whom are already demoralized by having already spent thousands of dollars on unsuccessful infertility treatments.

Let's discuss briefly the two traditional options currently available to prospective parents: international adoption and domestic adoption.

INTERNATIONAL ADOPTION

The adoption of children from other countries is an increasingly popular option for today's prospective parents. In just the last decade, the number of international adoptions by Americans has tripled, from about 6,500 in 1992 to over 19,000 in 2001. Originally prompted by the consequences of war, international adoption was first practiced during World War II when U.S. citizens opened their homes and hearts to many European and Japanese war orphans. As wars later erupted in Korea and in Vietnam, adoptions from these countries followed. More recent, poverty and social upheaval have been cited as factors in the adoption of children from Latin America, the former Soviet Union, and Eastern Europe. Today, population control policies in China have transformed the country into the most popular source for children adopted internationally. Together with Russia, China currently accounts for nearly half of all international adoptions by Americans.

Hopeful parents turn to international adoption for many reasons. Most believe that the children awaiting homes are plentiful and once your agency's requirements are met, a successful adoption is virtually guaranteed. For this reason, they assume that international adoption can pose less financial risk than a domestic adoption. But this is not always the case. In a recent survey of international adoptive parents, 14 percent said their adoption cost more than the agency told them it would cost and 11 percent stated that overseas agency facilitators and representatives asked them to pay additional fees that were not previously disclosed by their agencies. Hopeful parents also continue to favor international adoption for philosophical reasons. As in earlier years, they wish to provide care and opportunities for children who otherwise may suffer a life of hardship.

However, international adoption also has several unique characteristics that can represent obvious disadvantages for some prospective parents. For example, because complexities in law and procedures can produce many delays, there are few opportunities to adopt a newborn. An adoptive parent must be willing and able to travel to the child's country of origin and remain there for extended periods of time, which can often prove difficult and expensive. In addition, people considering international adoption are sometimes concerned about the health of the available children. Medical and other background information about the biological parents can be limited or unavailable. Poor health and environmental conditions in many countries can adversely impact a child's physical and emotional well-being. At times, children who have been born healthy will languish in orphanages that lack healthy stimulation and interaction. As a result, developmental delays can occur. In other cases, "attachment" problems arise, making it difficult for children to bond with their new parents. With these issues in mind, some prospective parents decide to investigate domestic adoption.

DOMESTIC ADOPTION

Those who wish to adopt a baby in the United States must generally decide between two common routes. One method is to use an agency, either public or private. Public agencies are government-operated, and are frequently part of a state's Social Services Department. Although one advantage of public agency adoption is the relatively low cost, many of these agencies have few, if any, newborns available. According to the U.S. Department of Health and Human Services, only 2 percent of waiting children are less than one year old. People who wish to adopt a newborn through a public agency are often dismayed to learn that the expected wait is between seven and nine years from the time the home study is completed. For them, private adoption agencies offer another, albeit more expensive, option.

For years, private adoption agencies were the traditional choice for those seeking to adopt an infant. Placements were often made on a first-come, first-served basis. The agency played a central role, both in matching birth and adoptive parents and in addressing the often complex and changing needs of all involved. However, over time, clients began to voice dissatisfaction over the restrictions and policies of some agencies. One problem was the unwillingness to place a baby with a couple until the birth parents' rights had ended. This meant that the child was placed in foster care for a period of time following his or her birth. Understandably, both sets of parents usually preferred to have the baby go home with the adoptive parents directly from the hospital. In addition, some adoptive parents and birth parents avoided using agencies because of what they perceived to be unnecessary bureaucratic red tape and interference. Fortunately, the private agency scene has evolved in recent years. Many agencies have altered their policies to better meet the needs of all their clients—adoptive parents, birth parents, and child. For example, both sets of parents are now encouraged to participate actively in the placement process. Some agencies allow a baby to go home with the adopting parents straight from the hospital. Despite this, some drawbacks still exist. Chief among them is the length of time applicants must wait if they are seeking to adopt a newborn. Couples must occasionally wait five or more years to complete a domestic infant agency adoption.

The other common method of domestic adoption is called independent or nonagency adoption. Independent adoptions can be conducted in one of two ways. Adopting parents can ask an attorney or other intermediary to help them locate a birth mother. Intermediaries may be friends, clergy members, physicians, attorneys, licensed social workers, or adoption consultants. Or, adoptive parents can actively seek a birth mother themselves, and rely on professionals to help screen candidates and coordinate details. In both cases, an attorney must be hired to advise on legal issues and to prepare the necessary legal documents. Sometimes called private adoption, independent adoption is currently legal in all but a few states. According to the National Adoption Information Clearinghouse, independent adoption is currently legal in all states except Connecticut, Delaware, Massachusetts, and Minnesota. However, in these states, the adoptive parents and the birth parents may identify each other without using an agency and then arrange parental rights to be relinquished through an agency later on. A unique advantage to independent adoption is the greater control both sets of parents have in making their adoption plans. Without an agency's interference, birth parents and adopting parents have a greater voice in making key decisions, often resulting in a better "fit" for everyone involved. On the other hand, while some adopters may prefer the flexibility of independent adoption, others believe this route is too expensive or too risky. In fact, both agency and independent adoption share several potential drawbacks.

Disadvantages to Domestic Adoptions

Risk
Regardless of the method of adoption you choose, there will be some risks. However, the actual risks involved are often different than what is popularly believed. Sensationalized media reports have led many to the conclusion that a birth parent can easily take the baby back once an adoption is complete. As such, there is a common belief that there is no guarantee that an adoption will remain

intact over time. In reality, this perception is incorrect. Each state specifies a set of adoption statutes that must be satisfied before an adoption is considered legal. Once all legal requirements are met, the adoption becomes final. Although cases exist where adoptions have been dissolved or contested after finalization, these occurrences are rare. Statistics show that less than 2 percent of adoptions are dissolved after finalization, and even fewer, 1 percent, are ever legally challenged. Another common belief is that a birth parent who has access to an adoptive family's information will become intrusive and demanding once the baby is placed. Adopting parents worry that a birth mother will encroach on their lives, making endless, inappropriate demands to see her child. For example, they may fear that a birth mother will show up unannounced on their doorstep for Thanksgiving. Fortunately, this scenario is the rare exception. In cases where birth parents know the identity of the adopting family, most are respectful of the boundaries and conform to arrangements mutually agreed upon in advance. In addition, most are concerned about their child's future well-being and are generally reluctant to do anything to jeopardize his or her adjustment within the adoptive family. In fact, knowing about the adopting family prior to the placement can assist a birth mother in her grieving process by reassuring her that she has made the right choice.

Although some fears are misplaced, domestic adoption does have risks—financial risks, risks related to the child's health, risks associated with the birth parent's level of commitment to the adoption plan, and risks associated with poor or inadequate adoption planning. Adoption expenses for both agency and independent adoptions can be quite high and do not come with any guarantee of a successful adoptive placement. Since many of the costs involved in adoption may be nonrefundable, things can get very expensive when an adoption falls through. In such cases, adoptive families must often cope with a considerable loss of funds in addition to the heartbreak of losing a child.

There will also be risks associated with the health of the child. Adoptive parents are unlikely to learn everything about the medical and social backgrounds of the birth parents. At the same time, even with adequate information, future medical problems in the child cannot always be predicted in every case. Whenever possible, adoptive parents should receive accurate information about the baby they seek to adopt in order to assist their decision making, reduce their chances of being "surprised" with serious undisclosed problems, and prepare them to parent more effectively.

Risks are also associated with the planning of the proposed adoption. Once a birth mother match is found, numerous details must be coordinated in order for the adoption to proceed successfully. The adoption planning must not only meet the expectations of both sets of parents but must also comply with legal requirements as well. Only the most experienced adoption professionals can successfully shepherd the process through to a conclusion that is satisfactory for all parties. Adoptive parents who rely on professionals who are not up to the task may be forced to watch helplessly as their dream slowly unravels.

The Wait

One of the biggest fears facing those who seek to adopt a baby is that of the well-known, interminable wait. Finding the right birth mother often takes time. Would-be parents who rely on agencies, attorneys, or other intermediaries can achieve a successful match within a year, but not always. Expertise and qualifications vary broadly among adoption arrangers. In fact, one of the biggest problems facing prospective adopters is that they often cannot know how effective an agency or intermediary really is at connecting with birth mothers until they have engaged their services and paid at least some of their fees. As Mary Lib Mooney of the adoption watchdog group Adoption Advocates of America states, "It can be very difficult to know just how many birth mothers an attorney, facilitator, or agency really has. For example, an agency may present itself as being very active when in reality they have four hundred adoption applicants and only ten birth mothers. There is no way for prospective adoptive families to know for sure." Unfortunately, a long waiting period not only prolongs the realization of your dreams to parent, but contributes to a great deal of stress and accompanying physical and emotional symptoms. The Wait has been so engrained into popular adoption culture that some adoption books devote whole chapters on how to survive it. And then there are the prospective parents who wait for years only to be offered a "risky" adoption scenario. If that situation proves unsuccessful, trying again means waiting again. This can make the adoption journey seem like a never-ending, vicious circle. Given these factors, it's no wonder so many people get discouraged when they imagine adopting a baby through traditional avenues.

THE FAST TRACK METHOD—
A PROACTIVE ALTERNATIVE

Hopeful parents often feel they have little chance of fulfilling their desire for a newborn. It is widely believed in this country that you must be a celebrity, "know" somebody in the business, or be prepared to wait years if you want to adopt a newborn. Fortunately, these discouraging perceptions of domestic adoption are not entirely accurate. It is estimated that 2 percent of unmarried women place their children, many of them newborns, for adoption in the United States. Of the 3.5 million U.S. babies born annually, about 24,000 were placed for adoption. There are a great many women in this country who would like to arrange an adoption plan for their unborn babies, and they are often just as baffled as you are about where to begin.

Parents can become proactive by taking the lead in their own adoptions. For years, prospective adopters have used a variety of "networking techniques" to get the word out about their desire to connect with a possible birth mother. These include telling friends and family and distributing cards, flyers, and letters. Some techniques however, are more effective than others. Many adoption experts believe that the most effective networking technique is direct advertising, which is a key step in the Fast Track Approach. This book examines the use of adoption advertising along with two other keys to a faster, safer adoption. These are:

1. *Open communication* between both sets of prospective parents *prior* to committing to the adoption plan

2. *Close coordination* among all parties to the adoption (adopting parents, birth parents, and competent adoption professionals)— right from the earliest stages of adoption planning

3. *Adoption advertising* to quickly locate potential birth mother candidates

OPEN COMMUNICATION

Simply stated, you cannot have an adoption without a birth mother. However, much more is needed than *just* a birth mother.

You must find the *right* birth mother for *you*. Both you and your birth mother must share a common vision and be mutually satisfied with the details of the proposed plan. And most important, your birth mother must have sufficient confidence in her decision to proceed with the plan through finalization. How, then, can a hopeful parent meet the right birth mother? In traditional open adoptions, adopting parents wait while an adoption professional or agency searches for a pregnant woman who meets the applicant's general expectations. Once found, she is presented with relevant information about the adoption applicant. In most cases, a birth mother will be presented with more than one applicant so she has several potential families from which to make her selection. If the potential birth mother expresses an interest in an applicant, a meeting or other form of communication is often arranged between both sets of prospective parents. Adoptive and birth parents do most of their communicating *after* they have committed to each other. Although many adoptions are successfully completed in this fashion, others develop unpleasant surprises that are only detected later on. In this event, the adopting parents' only options are to proceed despite the problems or to step away from the arrangement and abandon the adoption attempt. If they proceed, adopting parents must essentially "roll with the punches," enduring a stressful situation while they hope for a positive outcome. If adoptive parents are unwilling to proceed and, instead, opt out of the arrangement, they must then suffer the loss of time and money as well as considerable emotional heartbreak.

A better approach is to communicate with one or more candidates *before* a commitment is made. Although direct contact will not guarantee a risk-free adoption, it can add an additional degree of confidence for both sets of parents, enabling adoption plans to proceed more smoothly. In the process, both parties enhance their opportunity to achieve an appropriate match and a more satisfactory adoption overall.

. . .

CHRISTINE: *"We had one adoption attempt fall through before we successfully adopted our little girl. We were more successful with our second birth mother. We got her phone number from our attorney and spoke with her frequently. We didn't wait for our attorney to tell us when to call. We just took the initiative. I needed to be confident that this birth mom was comfortable with the adoption plan. My husband and I talk with her at least once a week. As the due date approached, we spoke even more often, sometimes every other day. We also exchanged lots of pictures. I think the frequent contact was reassuring not only for us but for her as well. We all had a much better understanding of what to expect. After a while, we developed a pretty good relationship. When our daughter was born, we didn't have to worry about what would happen. We already knew we would be successful."*

. . .

CLOSE COORDINATION

Many adopting parents show a reluctance to get personally involved in the search for their child's parents, preferring instead to delegate this important task to others. Some believe that by paying a fee, they will be relieved of the inconvenience of conducting the search themselves. Others are lured by promises of a quick match. However, by forfeiting their right to participate actively in this part of the adoption process, adopters risk being excluded from many critical aspects, including the vital information exchange process. Those who position themselves "outside the loop" are forced to observe from the sidelines without any ability to personally detect the little warning signs that may foreshadow bigger problems ahead. From this perspective, their only choice is to rely on secondhand reports from agency staff or intermediaries. Unfortunately, while many adoption workers are competent, some are not. Would-be parents who engage unscrupulous or incompetent attorneys, agencies, or other intermediaries have much to lose. As previously noted, some adoption professionals may claim to have access to many birth mothers, when in fact they do not. Others, either negligently or intentionally, may inadequately elicit or convey information that has a direct bearing on the suitability of a proposed match. For example, an inexperienced adoption worker may be unable to adequately assess the birth mother's commitment to the adoption plan or she may miss certain warning signs of possible problems. Potential medical challenges in the child may not be disclosed to adopting parents until after they have brought the baby home. In some of these cases, medical history is not properly investigated. Or, if significant information is known, adoption workers may discount its importance, believing that the child will simply "grow out of it" and that sharing complete information will prevent the child from finding a suitable home. In cases like these, difficulties can surface only after time, money, and emotions have all been invested.

Adoptive parents must hire competent adoption professionals and insist on close coordination between all parties from the earliest stages of the adoption right on through to completion. While they cannot be expected to know everything or detect every possible warning sign, they can strive to become actively engaged in the process. Adoptive parents must not assume everything is being taken care of. Instead, they should ask questions and expect frequent updates from both their professional team as well as the prospective birth parents. As Karen Lane points out, "A lot of the most important information comes in casual conversation between the birth mother and you or your attorney. The more contact the better." As with anything else, the smartest adoption consumers are the ones who do their home-work, stay informed, and participate in the process.

ADOPTION ADVERTISING

While most adopters know that the traditional approach is to wait while an intermediary searches for a potential match, some are sur-prised to learn that waiting is not a requirement of the domestic infant adoption process. While many have achieved success with word of mouth or with broadcast letters to doctors or clergy, the most effective way to connect with prospective birth mothers is to use direct advertising. Rather than targeting those who might be in a position to know a pregnant woman, adoption ads target the pregnant woman directly. As a result, advertisements placed in newspapers or online are known for getting particularly fast results. Couples who launch an effective advertising campaign can often reduce their wait by months or even years. And no one is more motivated to run an effective advertising campaign than prospec-tive parents who dream of adding a child to their lives. Until recently, many people did not even know that they were *allowed* to take an active role in the adoption advertising process. But not only is it legal in most states, it can often make the difference between whether or not you are successful in achieving your dream to adopt.

· · ·

LEANNE: *"We are working on our second adoption and, like the last attempt, we are using Internet advertising to search for a birth mother. Our son's birth mother found us through our Web site almost four years ago. That time around, we had a personal Web page through our agency and had also registered our Web page in various search engines. Now many people are networking via the Inter-*

net, so our responses are a bit slower than before, so we are considering using newspaper advertising as well.

. . .

WENDY: *"For our first adoption, we decided to be very proactive in our search for a birth mother. I didn't like the idea of waiting around. So we followed everyone's advice and tried hard to get the word out. Since we had no idea what would work, we basically tried everything we could think of. We printed flyers and hung them everywhere. Besides giving them to fellow employees, friends and family, we also mailed them to high schools, colleges, teachers and crisis pregnancy centers. The flyers were a lot of work and the cost of printing and mailing was fairly expensive as well. We really didn't start to get results until we tried direct advertising."*

ADVANTAGES OF THE
FAST TRACK METHOD

While employing Fast Track principles requires some investment of time, effort, and money, the benefits can be significant. The potential advantages are listed in the text that follows.

A Faster Adoption

By launching an effective advertising campaign, you can significantly reduce the time required to complete an adoption. It only takes a couple of weeks to create a Web site or for an adoption advertisement to appear in a newspaper. Once the ads are in place, you can start receiving responses immediately. The period of time from the start of your search to the time you bring home your baby can be a few short months.

A More Satisfactory Experience

By actively searching for a birth mother yourself, you will have substantially more control than if you allow someone else to find one for you. Because you will be receiving the initial calls from pregnant women, you can decide which leads to pursue and which ones to refer to others. Speaking to birth mothers directly will allow you to ask questions and hear her answers firsthand. This will allow you to collect more and better information than if you heard these answers paraphrased through an intermediary. In addition, you and your prospective birth mother can make some decisions directly without going through a third party. For example, when to speak next, whether you will exchange photographs, and what type of future contact you will maintain can all be discussed directly.

Getting personally involved in the adoption process can have significant benefits for those who wish to adopt. Contemporary psychology has repeatedly shown that having control over a desired outcome is associated with emotional well-being. For example, employees who are given greater personal control over their actions and decisions in the workplace experience higher levels of personal adjustment, mood, and task satisfaction. Even minor efforts at controlling one's problems can be satisfying. For example, merely making a telephone call to schedule an appointment with a therapist produces measurable emotional benefits. Having control not only boosts your emotional well-being but reduces physical symptoms. Conversely, people who are not in control of important parts of their lives are more likely to feel stress.

By maintaining their physical and emotional well-being, those would-be parents who get involved will be better prepared to organize and execute the necessary steps of an adoption. By contrast, those who fail to exercise some control over the adoption process may be burdened by stress and consequently be at a disadvantage.

Many adopters are also accustomed to experiencing control in other aspects of their lives. For them, it can be extremely frustrating to watch from the sidelines while others call the shots. In addition, a sense of control can appeal to infertile couples who, as Patricia Irwin Johnston points out in her book *Adopting After Infertility*, have not only lost control over their fertility but may have also surrendered their privacy and spontaneity during years of intrusive infertility treatments. Those who turn to adoption from infertility treatment are often relieved to direct their focus to those things that they can personally influence. In fact, active participation in adoption planning can be empowering—because the less stressed out you are, the better prepared you'll be for success.

Less Expense

By getting personally involved in selecting your birth mother, you can minimize the chance of proceeding with a risky adoption that could lead to a failed attempt. By achieving a good match the first time, you can potentially save thousands of dollars in unrecoverable birth mother expenses, medical expenses, and legal fees. In many cases, you will simply be combining your personal efforts with those of your adoption professionals to achieve a more thorough screening and selection process. As Laura Beauvais-Godwin and Raymond Godwin point out in *The Complete Adoption Book*, the candidate who speaks with you directly is more likely to be forced out of denial about adoption-related issues and may be better prepared to address the adoption plan more realistically. If not, she may continue to take advantage of financial assistance as she works through adoption issues at your expense.

Furthermore, taking charge during the early planning stages of your adoption is a smart way to protect yourself from being taken advantage of by unscrupulous adoption arrangers who offer to take the search for a birth mother off your hands in exchange for large fees. Some unethical attorneys, agencies, or other intermediaries lure couples desperate to adopt by promising to find them a baby. Unfortunately, couples sometimes part with thousands of dollars and wait years only to discover that there is no baby and no refund. Potential adoptive parents should be cautious of those who offer to do all the work for you in exchange for large up-front fees. They run the risk of waiting a long time for what could be a potential risky adoption situation. Or worse, they may be scammed.

The cost of advertising can be reasonable, especially when compared to the overall costs of an adoption. Although there is always the potential to spend an unlimited amount of money on adoption advertising, those who spend excessively usually do so because they lack an effective strategy. Although total costs will vary depending on the time allowed and methods used, when advertising is properly planned, it is possible to limit the total costs to $3,000. In many cases advertising can be done for substantially less. Compared to other types of networking, the cost of direct advertising is often comparable or only slightly higher.

Many people hire intermediaries to assist with matchmaking and adoption planning. But if you locate your own birth mother, you can avoid fees that can range from $3,000 to $12,000 or more.

Requires Only Moderate Effort

With the Fast Track approach, you will have to do very little yourself. In fact, your role is mainly to get the ball rolling. Once you locate a birth mother, your attorney or other adoption specialist will interview her and handle most of the necessary arrangements and details. Many of the things you will be required to do are those you would need to do for any domestic adoption—including choosing an attorney or agency, preparing an autobiographical profile, and completing a home study. The additional steps that you'll have to perform are relatively easy. Everything you need to know is clearly presented in this book.

The Option of Openness

The Fast Track approach incorporates a central feature of independent adoption called "openness." Open adoption means keeping the lines of communication open between the birth parents and adoptive parents. Although openness in adoption is a common feature of today's adoptions, this was not always the case. Past generations attached a stigma to adoption, and many families did their best to keep an adoption a well-guarded secret, often from the child himself. Unfortunately, children of closed adoptions would often learn the truth much later, which resulted in a sense of shame and betrayal. Furthermore, adopted children and their families frequently experienced later difficulties over the lack of available birth parent information, including social and medical histories.

Fortunately, this veil of secrecy is now being lifted. In open adoptions, both sets of parents experience some degree of contact. The precise amount of contact varies and is based on the desires of both sets of parents. In addition, in many open adoptions, the amount of contact may decrease following the child's placement. As such, openness is really a relative term and the openness of any given adoption is tailor-made to fit the preferences of both sets of parents. Most independent adoptions are open to some extent.

Finally, and most important, the children themselves benefit greatly from openness by learning more about their earliest beginnings. In this way, adoptive children will know that they joined the best adoptive family for them after much love and careful thought by all those involved.

. . .

HOLLY: *"Having placed two sons for adoption at their birth in a closed adoption system, I felt an incredible loss and separation. Had I been involved in the process by being aware and having choices of where my children had gone, with whom, and that they were thriving, I could have been more at peace. Although the closed adoption system of that time was very difficult on me, I have found peace and acceptance after many years. Talking to others in the adoption community has helped. I have also had the great fortune to meet and observe a case of an open adoption where the birth mother is kept informed. It appears to me to be a healthier solution."*

. . .

A Safer Adoption

Adequate information is essential before a decision can be made about a potential adoption situation. Unfortunately, in many adoptions that are arranged through intermediaries, the adoptive couple speaks with the birth mother only after both sets of parents have agreed to proceed. By this time, money, time, and emotions may have all been invested, making it harder to back out if the adoptive parents sense a possible problem.

But with the open, proactive approach, you will speak with the birth parents *before* a commitment is made. This will give you the opportunity to ask questions and learn as much as you can about the birth mother's family history, her prenatal care, or anything else that you may have concerns about. As a result, you will be much better prepared to make a more informed decision regarding the appropriateness of the proposed match.

Of all the reasons for you to get directly involved in the early planning stages of an adoption, perhaps the very best is because it is *your* adoption. Yet those eager to adopt have often been slow to fully participate in actions that can affect their lives forever. Whether lacking confidence or know-how, too many prospective adopters prefer to keep the adoption process at arm's length. By doing so, they are willing to defer on what may be the most critical decision of all—the selection of the woman who will give life to their most cherished dream.

If you are truly ready to adopt a child, why not take an active part right from the very beginning? After all, the adoption you are planning is not your attorney's adoption or your agency's. It's *your* adoption. Would you let someone else choose your spouse? If not, then why would you let another person assign you your child? Ultimately, this is about your life, your family, and your future.

2

STEP ONE: GET READY

Before a couple can pursue adoption, both partners must feel emotionally, mentally, and physically ready to adopt. They must confront certain realities regarding their marriage, health, finances, and lifestyle. And they must also identify their expectations for the adoption including their personal preferences and limits. For example, decisions must be made about the child they would like to adopt, the type of professional or agency they would like to use, and the amount of contact they would like with the birth mother. Above all, they must be ready to embrace adoption as the right solution for them, willing to do their homework and confident in their ability to succeed.

ARE YOU READY TO ADOPT?

Adoption specialists occasionally find that they locate a birth mother only to learn that the clients have changed their mind about proceeding with the adoption. In fact, some people who think they want to adopt are not completely ready. Those who question whether or not adoption is right for them will naturally hesitate to commit totally to the process, which will consequently limit their odds for success. Adoption can be a big step for many couples who have dreamed for years of having a biological child but are unable to conceive. Being psychologically ready to adopt means coming to terms with your infertility. Couples who have had a stressful experience with infertility treatment may feel too emotionally exhausted to pursue adoption, or they may worry that they will encounter even more disappointment. If you are considering adoption, the time to examine your feelings is *now*. Adoption situations can come up quickly, especially if effective networking techniques are used. Will you be emotionally ready when the time comes? The following questions are provided to help you assess your own readiness to adopt. If you have a partner, respond to the questions separately, then compare and discuss your answers afterward. Each partner should have the opportunity to explore his or her view openly and honestly.

Why do you wish to adopt? Many people are surprised by their answer to this question. For example, some may believe adopting a child will be a cure for existing marital difficulties, but it is always best to resolve such difficulties before proceeding down the path to adoption. Adopting a child is never a remedy for marital issues. Another motive often cited is the belief that adoption will lessen the pain of infertility. When infertility treatments fail, couples must face many losses including the loss of the family's genetic lineage, the loss of conceiving a child together, the loss of experiencing pregnancy and labor, and finally, the loss of the opportunity to parent a child. But adoption can remedy only one of these losses— the opportunity to parent. Couples who approach adoption after infertility must be certain that their foremost desire is to parent a child. If the primary goal is something other than becoming a parent, couples are likely to feel cheated out of their dreams and adoption will be viewed as second best or a last resort. Infertile couples who do not sufficiently acknowledge and resolve their losses will be ill-equipped to cope with the demands of the adoption process or, worse, may be disappointed with the eventual outcome, even if successful.

Another reason some choose adoption is to help troubled children by sharing their lives of privilege. While this desire is frequently cited among those who choose international adoption, it should not be the sole motive but rather one of several reasons to pursue adoption. However, if your only reason to adopt is humanistic or altruistic, there are better ways to contribute to the less fortunate. Of all the reasons to adopt a child, one of the best is simply to become a parent and share your life with a child whom you can love.

What are your options for starting or building your family? How do the advantages and disadvantages of other options compare to those of adoption? In deciding whether you are ready to adopt, most couples will review their options for starting or building their family. Advances in reproductive technology as well as changes in their social acceptability mean couples and singles have more options than ever before for bringing a child into their lives. Those who wish to conceive and birth a biological child may want to learn more about their medical treatment options. Many people today also consider using a third party, as with donor eggs or sperm. Plus, the use of surrogates continues to be a growing trend. Each of these routes to parenthood has its own set of advantages and disadvantages, including time, expense, physical discomfort, and risk. Therefore, it is essential to evaluate your options carefully. In some cases, it may be helpful to list the pros and cons associated with each.

How will your families feel? People considering adoption are often exposed to the attitudes and feelings of their family members, including parents, grandparents, older children, or other relatives. These attitudes can play a significant role in shaping one's decision to pursue adoption. It is not unusual for some family members to be ill-informed about adoption issues, particularly about how adoption works today. Some family members may have heard media reports of adoptive parents who have suffered a tragic loss and may feel the need to protect or discourage loved ones from experiencing a similar fate. In this case, prospective adopters can sometimes recruit their support by sharing accurate information to address these concerns or misconceptions. Fortunately, many family members will be enthusiastic about the prospect for a new family member through adoption. When this occurs, they can play a valuable supportive role by providing much-needed encouragement, especially during stressful times.

. . .

MARGIE: *"My husband and I were very lucky. Both sets of our parents were extremely supportive of our goal to adopt. I think it probably helped that they viewed this as one of the few ways they could have a grandchild, and in my parents' case, it was to be their first. Although everyone had a healthy concern for possible scenarios in which our adoption could unravel, for the most part their support was unwavering. Getting the green light from them was a real confidence booster and helped give us just a little extra momentum to see us through the long adoption process."*

. . .

Can you manage insensitive comments and questions? Adoptive parents often report that they and their children are the subject of unusual comments and questions from friends and family. The fact is that most people who have not personally experienced adoption do not have a particularly good understanding of it. This often results in remarks and questions that span the whole range from those that are basically harmless to some that can be quite cruel. Examples include: "Who is the baby's real mother?"; "How could she give the baby up?"; "Will the baby be taken away?"; "How much did you pay for her?"

In addition, people can often be oddly judgmental about one's efforts to adopt. As Jana Wolff points out in her book *Secret Thoughts of an Adoptive Mother*, there is often an unspoken belief that those seeking to adopt should be happy with any child they can get. Unlike other couples who start a family simply because they wish to be parents, adoptive parents must often conform to higher standard. As a result, the most personal adoption-related decisions can be open to value judgments and political or social interpretations. Common hot-button triggers include the child's ethnicity, health, age, or country of origin. While it is often considered more acceptable to desire an older or special-needs child, the fact is that almost any preference on the part of adoptive parents can be open to scrutiny.

And if you've adopted a dissimilar-looking child you all face additional challenges, as these families are apt to be noticed and remarked on in public. Although a child's adoption is a very personal matter, it is not always a private one. (Fortunately, over time, most adoptive parents learn to disregard odd stares and comments while reminding themselves that the average person has a long way to go in their understanding of adoption and adoptive families.)

. . .

LAUREN: *"I would have to say that most of the time people are very positive when they hear our kids are adopted. But sometimes people do say some strange things. Many times, people have told us how lucky our kids are to 'have us.' We don't feel that way at all. We think it's the other way around. And then my elderly aunt is convinced that we are 'saints' for taking in an orphan. We have tried to tell her that we are not saints. But she remains unconvinced and she continues to tell us this every time we talk to her. We hear a lot about our lack of physical resemblance, but we know comments like these are basically just small talk and can be even funny at times. However, some remarks have been very painful. Two people who know about our adoption story have said extremely hurtful things, and one of them was my best friend. She was going through a difficult pregnancy at the same time that we were trying to adopt our first child. She told a mutual acquaintance that my husband and I were having a child 'the easy way.' It makes me wonder what other people must be saying or thinking about us.*

. . .

How does parenting an adopted child differ from parenting a biological one? Even those who adopt a child at birth must confront certain issues that are unique to adoption. For example, regardless of how young they are at the time of placement, adopted children will always have a previous history. This fact will often become an enduring theme once they are able to understand the more complex issues behind the adoption process, generally around the age of seven or eight. Many adopted children have difficulty resolving identity issues or struggle with doubts stemming from their relinquishment. In fact, the adoptive family will always be linked to the birth family, even if contact is minimal or nonexistent. Adoptive parents who acknowledge these issues from the outset will be better prepared to understand and support their children if later problems arise.

How will you feel if your child later chooses to search for or meet with his or her birth parents? Once adopted children are developmentally equipped to understand the complex issues of adoption, many will desire to know more about their origins and some will seek a reunion with their birth parents. Some adoptive parents view this as a threat to their parent-child relationship, while others are secure in their roles as parents and work constructively to meet the needs of their children. Take some time now to reflect on how you would meet this challenge. By preparing now, you can begin to anticipate issues and lay the foundation for a healthy resolution for all concerned.

Will you be able to love and bond with a nonbiological child? This question is perfectly understandable. It is common for people to worry about whether they can love an adopted child or if the child will love them in return. After all, becoming parents through adoption requires a certain "leap of faith." Those new to parenting may have the greatest fears of all. For those struggling with this question, it may be reassuring to know that in the overwhelming majority of cases, parents not only love their adopted children but feel that they were absolutely "meant to be." Although attachment can develop at different rates for different parents, most adoptive parents eventually develop a strong bond with their children. Most feel that it would be impossible to love these children any more than they do and cannot imagine their lives without them.

DAVE: *"Before we adopted Chase, I really agonized over how much I would love an adopted child. It was the number one question for me. I really had my doubts, and for a while it was the only thing that was holding me back from jumping in."*

CAROL: *"I think you started getting cold feet even after we decided to go for it. I sensed that you were questioning things a lot more as we got closer to the due date."*

DAVE: *"I was pretty nervous."*

CAROL: *"As for me, I was the one who was convinced that adoption was the way to go. I didn't feel any of the same doubts at all. I felt very confident that our decision to adopt was the right thing for us. And I also thought that I would bond with an adopted child just as much as I would with a biological one. So I guess it's a little funny how we reacted to Chase after his birth."*

DAVE: *"Right up until his birth, I was questioning everything. But guess what? The minute I held him in my arms, all those doubts flew right out the window. It was almost instantaneous."*

CAROL: *"As confident as I was going into the adoption, I was a bit surprised that it took me a while to bond. In fact, I distinctly remember that for the first two weeks, I felt like I was babysitting somebody else's child."*

DAVE: *"Having gone through the process I can honestly say that there is no way that I could love a child any more, even if I had gone the biological route. I managed to figure this out myself. That was really the hardest part—I wish someone could have told me all this before. It's almost embarrassing to think that I had those earlier doubts."*

CAROL: *"The love I now feel for Chase is absolute and fierce. If a fly lands on him, I feel like ripping it to shreds. It's totally impossible for me to love him any more. He definitely feels like a part of me. I feel so close to Chase that I sometimes have to remind myself that I didn't actually give birth to him. It's startling to think that I didn't."*

DAVE: *"We had a pretty nice life before we started a family. But looking back on it now, our life then was like in black and white. It's all in Technicolor now. I thank God every day for Chase. What would we ever do without him?"*

Can you handle the uncertainty of adoption? The process of adoption is an extremely fluid one. Information about the birth parents is often incomplete or pieced together from a variety of sources. The picture that is presented at the outset of the process is often painted with very broad strokes. Details are added as more information becomes available. Additionally, much of the information that is collected about a birth mother or father is obtained directly from that person alone and with little opportunity for independent verification. Emergencies arise and facts change. Your birth mother will provide you with information, and your adoption professional will provide you with more information. But the picture will almost always change. Adoptions are unpredictable and adopters must be willing and able to cope with a certain degree of uncertainty. They must also be willing to accept the fact that they may never have all the answers to their questions, even after the adoption is complete.

How will you feel if your adopted child turns out to have a disabling condition after the adoption is finalized? Those considering adoption have a right to be concerned about prenatal factors that may affect an adopted child's later development. While some medical conditions can be detected at birth, others may not present until years later. Although parents of biological children generally have better control over prenatal factors, there are some things that adoptive parents can do as well. First, it is important to remember that most birth mothers are also concerned for the future health of their unborn children. In addition, frequent preplacement contact between adoptive and birth parents often creates a very trusting relationship, which can more easily allow the exchange of questions and suggestions. Adopting parents who play an active role in the adoption process are also likely to receive more information about prospective birth parents, including health-related information. Finally, as adoptive parents, you do have the right to choose which medical problems you are willing to accept and which ones you cannot. Ultimately, it's important to remember that children do not come with medical guarantees, and when considering life with a child, we all must accept a certain degree of risk—whether we've adopted or not.

Will you be willing to comply with the recommendations of the home study worker? Adoption workers who conduct home study evaluations occasionally offer recommendations to their adoption applicants. In some cases, these recommendations may be requirements for a home study to be approved. In others, they are simply suggestions. For example, an applicant may be asked to remove a pet deemed inappropriate for young children. Or there may be a recommendation to make changes to your house to address safety concerns. Some of the more frequent suggestions include: taking a parenting course, reading up on adoption issues, or attending support groups. Your willingness to comply with recommendations is often a reflection of your commitment to the adoption process. One way to gauge your readiness to adopt, therefore, is to ask, "To what extent would I be willing to comply with an evaluator's recommendations?"

Will you be willing to comply with specific birth parent requests regarding child rearing, if any arise? Birth parents occasionally select their baby's adoptive family based on the type of care or opportunities they can provide. For example, it may be very important to them that one parent remain at home to care for the child full time. Or they may request private or higher education, specific religious instruction, or opportunities for travel. In some cases, the birth parent will ask to select the child's name. Which request or requests would you be willing to honor?

Do you have sufficient financial resources to commit to an adoption? Various factors can influence the overall cost of a domestic infant adoption. Some adoptions are considerably less expensive than others. Adopting parents often assist the birth mother with her medical and legal expenses. In some cases, they may also contribute money for her rent, counseling, or maternity clothes. However, birth mothers who are employed or live with their parents may have relatively few financial needs. Some birth mothers may have their own medical insurance or can qualify for a program funded through their state. Adoption costs can also be kept at a minimum if the time between a birth mother's initial contact and her due date is brief, for example, weeks rather than months. Adoption fees are generally not paid up front or all at once. And assistance is available to adopting families through employer adoption benefits, military subsidies, and federal tax credits. (See chapter 3 for more information on planning a realistic adoption budget.)

How far are you willing to travel? Are you willing to adopt a baby born only in your state, in neighboring states, or anywhere in the United States? While traveling out of state to adopt can add to your overall adoption expenses, your chances for a timely and suitable match increase as your geographical "net" expands.

Are you willing to invest the time and energy needed to learn about adoption? Those who wish to adopt successfully must be prepared to make a series of decisions—decisions that must be well informed and carefully considered. Among the adoption professionals who are available to assist, many are experienced and qualified, while some are not. Often it is hard to tell the two groups apart. Adopters who get into trouble are frequently those who fail to do their homework before proceeding with their plans to adopt. Fortunately, there are good resources to help prospective parents. Advocacy groups such as Adoptive Families of America, National Adoption Information Clearinghouse, and RESOLVE offer valuable publications in the form of magazines and fact sheets (see the appendix). Adoption consultants are also available to meet with you to explain various options and their relative merits. But perhaps the best resource of all is talking with others who have recently adopted. Support groups, available in many cities across the country, are specifically designed to provide forums for those who wish to exchange their questions and experiences about the adoption process. Those considering adoption are strongly advised to explore this valuable resource (see the appendix).

. . .

AMY: *"When my husband and I made the decision to pursue adoption, I made every effort to learn all I could about the process. I made countless phone calls to adoptive parents, took a class called Adoption Insights, read several books on adoption, started a subscription to* Adoptive Families Magazine, *and talked*

(continued on page 42)

HOW TO USE THE INTERNET FOR
ADOPTION INFORMATION

The Internet can be an invaluable tool for those who wish to educate themselves about adoption. In recent years, the amount of available adoption-related information has virtually exploded. Today, there are newsgroups (maintained by special interest groups on a variety of adoption-related topics), magazines, e-mail groups, chat forums, bulletin boards, and numerous organizations dedicated to adoption advocacy, education, support, and research. Dozens of Web sites offer information on statistics, getting started, legal issues, open adoption, networking, and more. In many cases, one Web site will provide links to other ones. Using these links, you can send messages, request information, and download applications, fact sheets, articles, and even books. Once you get started, it may be difficult to stop. One way to access adoption information on the Internet is to use one of the major search engines (see the appendix). You will find hundreds of sites by simply typing in key search words such as *child adoption* or *open + adoption*. Another good way to learn about Internet resources is to contact the National Adoption Information Clearinghouse (see the appendix) and ask for *The Adoption Guide to the Internet.*

While a wealth of information is available on the Internet, it is important to observe a few precautions. Consider the following questions:

What Is the Source of the Information?

Web sites can be maintained by nonprofit organizations, individuals, agencies, registries, facilitators, or attorneys. Some sites offered by nonprofit organizations are a solid source of accurate information. But not all. Just because a site looks authoritative, it doesn't necessarily mean that the information provided is accurate and up-to-date. Conversely, sites that appear very commercial with numerous paid advertisements may actually offer a wealth of legitimate information. Never accept any information as true simply because it appears on the Internet. Evaluate the information provided by checking to see if references are provided. If not, the material may simply be a matter of opinion and not based on objective measures. As Chris Adamec points out in her book *The Complete Idiot's Guide to Adoption*, individuals often use the Internet to promote their personal opinions about adoption issues. In other cases, a Web site may contain one-sided information designed to benefit a commercial venture. Subtle forms of advertisements are often presented as fact. Try to determine the purpose of the site. Is it to inform or to sell? Legal issues should always be checked with your adoption attorney.

How Current Is the Information?

Many people mistakenly assume that simply because the information is on the Internet, it must be recent. In reality, information can remain there for years. Look to see if the posted information is dated. If not, do not assume it is current.

Who Are the People You Are Communicating with On-line?

People interested in a common topic are often drawn to forums, chat rooms, or adoption e-mail lists. In some cases, participants are asked to subscribe by sending a message to an e-mail address. Others use the Internet to reach out to adoption experts featured on one of many Web sites. If you are inclined to connect with others this way, exercise extreme caution. Things on the Internet are not always who or what they seem. It is difficult to really know anyone you meet on-line. Be wary of those who claim to be facilitators and offer to help you for a fee. Be cautious when sharing information with prospective adoptive parents or others who seem to share your situation—remember that they may not really be quite as similar as you think. And do not form opinions or base your decisions solely on what you have heard from others on-line. If you decide to post questions or comments, remember that your privacy is not guaranteed on the Internet. All of the information you provide, including your name, address, and personal details about yourself, can be viewed and shared by anyone who logs on. In addition, the information can remain available for years.

(continued from page 39)

about adoption to anyone who would listen to me! These things really helped me stay focused on our goal and also kept me busy in my spare time. Looking back on the experience, the books, magazines, and talking to adoptive parents were most helpful in educating us as to what we were getting ourselves into."

. . .

Are you willing to invest the time and energy to actively participate in the adoption process from start to finish? Like many areas of life, little adoption problems often have a way of becoming bigger unless promptly addressed. By remaining out of touch with the proceedings, adopting parents risk encountering an unpleasant surprise only after it is too late to do anything about it. By contrast, actively involved adopting parents have a much greater opportunity to exchange information, receive feedback, and monitor developments. As a result, they stand a much greater chance of deterring potential problems and achieving the kind of tailor-made adoption that is right for them.

Once you have considered these questions, it's time to compare your answers with your partner, if you have one. One person's concern may frequently be quite different from the other's. Do not worry if you differ on some of the finer points. In fact, it is very unusual for couples to agree on everything about adoption. Don't forget that biological parents commonly have differences and yet proceed with family building anyway. It is important, however, to agree on the major issues such as the particular route to pursue, the degree of openness desired, and most of all, the belief that adoption is the best choice. Where concerns or fears exist, recruit the assistance of adoptive couples who have encountered similar difficulties. Or consider meeting with a qualified adoption counselor to seek resolution in a therapeutic setting.

READINESS TO EMPLOY THE FAST TRACK METHOD

Having the right attitude is important for anyone wishing to adopt, but it is essential for those who wish to use proactive strategies to adopt quickly. In a traditional adoption, prospective parents are guided though the process. But a Fast Track adoption requires you to be sufficiently mentally and emotionally prepared to take the lead.

Personal Attributes of Fast Track Adopters

Prospective parents who employ proactive strategies to adopt quickly and safely usually share similar characteristics. They are more likely to be:

Committed
Using networking strategies, including advertising, means that the prospective parents are "getting the word out" about their desire to adopt. While couples who pursue a traditional adoption need only to admit their infertility to themselves and their professional helpers, those who advertise for a birth mother must also be willing to publicize their infertility to the outside world. In other words,

they must be willing to make a public commitment. Demonstrating a public commitment often has a positive effect on the eventual outcome. Research has shown that people are more likely to follow through on plans if they announce their intentions to others. For example, smokers who tell others of their plans to quit are more likely to be successful. Conversely, those who avoid a public commitment may do so because they feel uncertain about their desire for change.

Confident

Fast Track adopters believe in their ability to organize and execute the necessary demands of a prospective adoption. They believe that they have the personal competence required to achieve success. Much of contemporary psychology has recognized the importance of confidence as a crucial element of success. For example, people tend to engage in tasks in which they feel competent and confident and avoid those in which they do not. And once the initial goal is set, those who believe in their ability to succeed are more likely to expend energy and to persist in the face of obstacles. Consequently, those who expect success in their goal to adopt are more likely to be successful. The opposite is true of those who lack such confidence.

Unfortunately, confidence may be in short supply for couples who pursue adoption after infertility treatment. Years of failure have often taught them to lower their expectations of what they can accomplish. It often takes time to make the important realization that adoption is different. The vast majority of people who seriously pursue adoption are ultimately successful. Refocusing one's attention from infertility treatment to adoption often requires a change of perspective. Those who find it difficult to shift gears should consider adoption counseling. A few sessions can be helpful in processing the losses of the past and ensuring that these experiences do not interfere with future attempts to adopt successfully.

Analytical and Informed

Attitudes about adoption are frequently formed on the basis of stereotypes, fear, or hearsay. Conclusions may be arrived at in haste without a thorough understanding of the facts. At times, the media has also contributed to the problem. Adoption stories in the press are usually about the cases that somehow go wrong. The fact that most adoptions are completed successfully often goes unnoticed. Unfortunately, popular perceptions about adoption have been shaped by these negative portrayals. Prospective adopters who embrace unrealistically negative adoption attitudes can inadvertently sabotage their chances for success. By contrast, successful adopters counteract sensational anecdotes by availing themselves of accurate information and helpful resources before they proceed. They recruit experts, request brochures, and join support groups. They do not accept hearsay or media reports as fact, but seek out the truth about controversial topics. In doing so, they challenge their own fears and preconceived notions and are better prepared to make informed decisions based on fact.

Assertive and Involved

Fast Track adopters are asserting themselves and their right to be happy. They believe they deserve to be successful, and are willing to take charge of their lives, engaging fully in the adoption experience.

Organized

Fast Track adopters are able to organize information from a variety of sources. They are good at taking notes and keeping records. They follow up on all leads, large or small.

SET UP A FILING SYSTEM

Fortunately, those new to adoption can take advantage of a bounty of adoption information from many different sources. Articles are available from support groups, magazines, newspapers, and Internet sites. You are also likely to receive literature from agencies, attorneys, and other adoption professionals. While the availability of information can be very helpful to prospective adopters, many are caught off guard by the small torrent of fact sheets, forms, pamphlets, receipts, and other material they acquire after only a few brief inquiries. Snowball-like, this growing quantity of paperwork will continue to expand until your adoption is finalized and your house is bulging. As the months go by, there will be many times when you will wish to find some small item quickly. If adoption information is not organized in some coherent fashion, you may experience hours of unnecessary searching. Save yourself time and frustration by setting up some files now, before the influx begins. One of your most important files will be one marked "Receipts." Carefully document *all* adoption expenses, including those related to: travel, car rental, hotel, meals, books, applications, memberships, subscriptions, counseling, legal, and birth mother assistance. Save all canceled checks. You may also wish to label other files for: Adoption Fraud, Agencies, Attorneys, Counseling, General Information, Internet Resources, Legal Information, Our Profile, and Sample Adoption Ads.

Persistent

Fast Track adopters view potential obstacles as challenges to overcome and are resolved to persevere. If one avenue is not fruitful, they try another one. Even those who experience a failed adoption can succeed if they persist. In fact, the question is often not if they will be come a parent, but when.

. . .

SARA: *"Before we were finally successful, we experienced one adoption that unraveled at the last minute. Our birth mother changed her mind a week before she was due. I was devastated. I didn't know if I would ever stop thinking about that baby. But most of all, I remember feeling very fatalistic, as though we had lost our only chance. At the time, it didn't occur to me that we could try again. But after a while, I realized that we could afford another attempt. After that, I was a lot less panicky. I realized that we were good candidates, that we had a lot to offer a child, and that we would eventually be successful—it was only a matter of time. I think having this attitude really helped me survive emotionally. We were successful on the second attempt."*

. . .

Resilient
Very few adoptions go smoothly from start to finish. Many adoptions that are ultimately successful experience at least some difficulties along the way. Fast Track adopters accept this fact and can recover quickly when minor setbacks occur.

Focused
Parents who adopt quickly are focused on the ultimate goal of bringing their baby home. They try to keep the big picture in mind and do not allow themselves to become derailed by unexpected bumps in the road.

Decisive
Opportunities can appear as soon as ads are in place. Fast Track adopters are prepared to act quickly. Because they have done the necessary mental preparation in advance, they are able to recognize a good possibility and respond immediately.

Realistic and Flexible

They are aware of the complex nature of adoption and allow for the possibility that they may ultimately be very happy with an adoption situation that differs somewhat from what was originally envisioned. They understand that adoption issues are rarely black and white, and when they are uncertain about a particular course of action they make decisions by weighing the relative advantages and disadvantages. They acknowledge a difference between their fantasy adoption and the world as it really is. They realize that they may have to adjust their thinking and expectations. They think carefully before saying no to potential leads. They accept the fact that complete information just may not be available and are willing to make that leap of faith when necessary. After all, bringing a child into your life will always require a leap—and this is true for any child.

DECISIONS TO MAKE
ABOUT YOUR ADOPTION

Prospective parents can prepare themselves by making some decisions regarding the adoption they wish to pursue. Although adopting parents cannot select their baby, they do have a say when it comes to the baby's birth parents and their circumstances. Often, they will have certain requirements and limits on what they will accept. These are often referred to as one's "criteria" for the adoption. Some criteria will be rather more objective than others. For example, your budget may place some limits on the adoption situation you will accept. Other criteria will be identified only by searching your soul to discover what feels right for you.

While some adopters have at least one requirement that they feel they must insist upon, others may have criteria that are not requirements but rather, preferences. Once an appropriate birth mother is located, the sum of the available information is usually weighed in deciding whether or not to proceed. The general rule of thumb is to be as flexible as you possibly can. Most professionals agree that the more "open" you are with respect to your preferences and limitations, the wider the net you can cast. And the wider your net is, the greater your chances will be to adopt, and to adopt quickly. Simply because a pregnant woman has different qualities than what you had expected does not mean that she wouldn't make a wonderful birth mother. Whenever possible, couples should try to set aside their preferences on one point in order to proceed with an adoption situation that appears to have other advantages. Many successful adoptions occur only after the hopeful parents are able to relax one or more of their rules. If you get to know a pregnant woman who appears absolutely wonderful in every way except for the fact that she smokes cigarettes, it may be to your advantage to bend your rule about no drugs or alcohol. While having limitations and requirements may be important in making a situation comfortable for you, they also restrict your options. Try to limit your criteria to essentials only. Identify anything that you absolutely cannot accept and try to stay as open as possible to the different situations you may encounter.

Allow for the possibility that your attitudes may, and probably will, shift slightly over time. This will be particularly true as you gain a greater understanding about birth parents and the adoption process in general. For example, you may initially believe that you will rule out any who appear stressed. However, as your adoption journey proceeds, you are likely to learn an important truth—that, in fact, due to the dynamics of the situation, most birth mothers *are* stressed. Also, make a point to check with your spouse on a regular basis and to reevaluate your expectations as the process unfolds.

Above all, try to be realistic. When considering your criteria, remember that there may be a difference between your fantasy child and what the real world can offer. One on-line parent registry worker described a client who complained of not receiving any responses in a full year of advertising. When questioned further, it was revealed that in fact she had heard from, and turned down, several possible birth mothers. She just had not discovered the one who matched perfectly with her many requirements (including no alcohol consumption either during *or at any time prior to* the pregnancy). While it's nice to dream, try to be open-minded, realistic, and willing to embrace the unexpected. Many happy adoptive parents will tell you that the circumstances of their child's adoption differed significantly from what they had originally envisioned. Avoid trying to adopt "the perfect child."

As a general guide, consider the following aspects to help you determine your personal criteria for adoption.

The Child

Ethnic Background
Those who feel that they could only accept a child of a particular race should ask themselves if they might not also be able to love one of another race or combination of races.

Health
Many people think that they will only accept a healthy baby. However, it is extremely important to define just what healthy means. For example, a baby can be healthy in every way except for a small correctable problem, such as a cleft palate or lip. Would you accept a minor, correctable birth defect? Although many adopters envision a healthy baby, most would not discontinue an adoption because

of a minor correctable problem. But, what if it's something more serious? Just where do you draw the line?

Some health problems are known prior to the baby's birth, while others are not. For example, a birth mother may tell you that a genetic illness runs in her family. If appropriate you could ask the mother to undergo an amniocentesis. Your decision to proceed can often be facilitated by doing some research on the condition to check for its possible severity and treatment options. If the baby may have a health problem that you do not feel comfortable with, it is best to acknowledge this to yourselves and your birth mother as soon as possible. In many cases, another home can easily be found.

Sex

Specifying the sex of the child as an absolute requirement is extremely tricky and generally not recommended. Those prospective parents who insist on adopting a child of a particular sex may wait considerably longer to achieve a suitable birth mother match. In fact, many adoption professionals who help locate birth mothers flatly state that they will not accept any requirements for sex. There are a few reasons for this. One, most pregnant women do not know the sex of their child prior to the birth. Certain prenatal tests that may reveal the fetus's sex may not be recommended unless it is deemed medically necessary. For example, amniocentesis is often used as a way to screen for potentially serious medical conditions; but because the test itself carries some risk of miscarriage, most doctors will not recommend it for expectant mothers younger than thirty-five years. Two, many children are identified as one sex prior to the birth, only to astonish everyone upon their arrival into the world. And finally, if a prospective birth mother learns that the adopting parents will accept only a girl, for example, where does that leave her (and her child) if she happens to deliver a boy? She will worry whether the child will still have a home. For this reason, many pregnant women will hesitate to select a couple who have a requirement for sex of the child. Remember that you have a 50-50 chance of getting the sex you want. After all, parents who build their family the old-fashioned way take their chances, too.

Intelligence

Some prospective parents hope to adopt a child with a strong potential for intellectual ability. But, like sex, intelligence is a difficult issue. You can try to interview the prospective birth parents, but how will you evaluate their intelligence? Even trained professionals have trouble assessing intelligence due, in part, to the fact that there are so many different types. But most of all, high native intelligence does not always predict actual intelligence. Many highly gifted individuals act unintelligently in real life. In fact, nurture (the environment in which a child is raised) often outweighs nature (what one is born with) in determining actual intelligence. This is good news for adoptive parents since they will provide the nurturing.

Other Factors

Children who have been conceived through rape or incest are occasionally placed for adoption. Be prepared for this possibility and ask yourself now how comfortable you would feel should this circumstance arise. As a final note, keep in mind that there's always a chance your birth mother could deliver multiple babies. You should consider your feelings about adopting more than one baby.

Birth Parents' Health and History

During your conversations with your birth mother, you will be in the position to elicit much of the information you seek regarding her health and personal history. In addition, she will also be interviewed by your adoption professional as well as her own obstetrician. In most cases, some of her medical records will be made available to you. The information that you receive about the birth parents may include such things as a physical description, religion, level of education, their reasons for considering adoption, due date of the baby, and whether the mother is receiving prenatal care. In addition, some information may also be collected describing medical work, social and criminal histories of the birth parents and their family. Although you are likely to receive health and background information from any birth mother you speak with, the same may not be true for the birth father. Some birth fathers simply cannot be identified. In other cases, the available information is very limited. Ask yourself now how you feel about receiving little or no information about a birth father.

Health

Most adopting couples are particularly interested in the birth mother's general health and access to proper medical attention. Many women who become pregnant unexpectantly, however, will not have seen a doctor before responding to adoption ads. In most cases, your adoption attorney will determine if the woman is receiving the proper care and will make the appropriate arrangements if necessary. Medical records or the birth mother's own self-report may reveal a family history of a certain condition. Doing some research will give you a better understanding of how the child may be affected. Prenatal tests can often be administered to detect the presence of these conditions in the unborn baby.

History

Most pregnant women who respond to adoption ads offer a physical description of themselves as well as a description of their circumstances, including: age, marital status, presence of other children, work status, level of education, and living arrangements. They may also include an explanation of why they are considering an adoption plan for their baby. Some women may state they are interested in adoption because raising a child simply conflicts with their goals for the future. However, others are experiencing a personal or financial crisis, and many of the women who respond to your ads will describe circumstances very different from your own. Some callers may have social or criminal histories that they will not disclose without being asked. However, it is often best to avoid asking callers directly about these sensitive subjects. Instead, your adoption attorney or other adoption professional can determine this type of information and report back to you. Prepare now by asking yourself how you would feel if a prospective birth mother was experiencing a financial crisis, has committed a criminal offense, or has experienced several unsuccessful marriages. How would you feel if the birth father had difficulty maintaining employment or was currently incarcerated? Keep in mind that while you may wonder what relationship a birth parent's circumstances might have to the future emotional health of the baby, the fact is that it is exceedingly difficult to predict a child's emotional or intellectual future simply on the basis of the birth parent's apparent difficulties. Problems that prompt women to choose adoption can be transitory in nature and often improve or resolve within a short period following the placement of the child. In other cases, factors that lead to the crisis may have nothing to do with a birth parent's native endowment, or the capabilities that person is bestowed with naturally. It is quite possible that a birth parent would be in very different circumstances if he or she had been provided with a different environment as a child.

Degree of Legal Risk

Private adoptions often vary according to their degree of legal risk. Risk can be influenced by many variables. As a result, most adoptions are evaluated on a case-by-case basis. One of the factors that can influence risk is the differences in state regulations describing conditions under which a birth mother may withdraw her consent and stop an adoption. For example, many states consider the adoption irrevocable once the birth mother has given her written consent. Another obvious factor to consider is the birth mother's commitment to the adoption plan. Fortunately, it is considered rare for a birth mother to change her mind and seek to reclaim her child after she has signed her consent. In fact, less than 1 percent of infant placements fail to become legalized adoptions. Most birth mothers who change their mind about the adoption do so before the child is placed in the adoptive home. Although it can be difficult to accurately estimate a prospective birth mother's commitment to an adoption plan, your adoption professional can assist by offering an assessment based on their experience. In addition, some of the factors that may influence commitment are discussed in chapter 8. Some situations regarding birth fathers may also be considered risky. Unknown fathers, those who cannot be located, and situations involving more than one possible father may carry an extra element of risk. Many pregnant women are not able to identify their baby's father and the majority of these adoptions proceed smoothly. Adoptions like these occur frequently. But, regulations concerning birth fathers' rights vary from state to state and certain cases, in some jurisdictions, can be risky or even dangerous. For this reason, prospective parents must consult with their attorney in order to understand the legal rights of all parties involved. As possible birth mothers are located, your attorney will explain the potential risks in greater detail based on the facts presented in each case. Until then, prospective parents can prepare by accepting the fact that all adoptions come with at least some degree of risk. While few ethical adoption professionals will encourage you to accept a case deemed very risky, some of the situations may be judged riskier than others. Would you consider only cases with minimal risk or can you tolerate moderate levels of risk?

Financial Assistance

This issue can be a touchy one for many seeking to adopt. Although state laws vary, most permit some birth mother assistance by adopting parents. Nevertheless, those birth mothers who ask for assistance are sometimes viewed with suspicion. Adopting parents worry that they may be faced with demands for ever-increasing amounts of money. In fact, most states limit assistance to those expenses deemed pregnancy-related. By relieving some of the stress during what can be a very difficult time, assistance can contribute to the health of both the birth mother and her unborn child. Paying allowable expenses can help some adoptions proceed more smoothly. At the same time, it is not unusual for birth mothers to be ashamed of their circumstances and to hesitate to ask for money. Before embarking on your advertising campaign, consider your own feelings with respect to this important issue. It may help to evaluate proposed situations on a case-by-case basis. However, in any event, financial assistance should be secondary in importance to the main goal of determining the right match between birth and adoptive parents and the best possible future for the child. Because restrictions on financial assistance vary from state to state, adopting parents who have ethical concerns over financial support can choose to focus their advertising on those states with the most restrictive laws.

Birth Parent Contact

Although your feelings about birth parent contact are likely to evolve as you proceed down the adoption path, it is important to start preparing now. Consider how much contact you would like to have with your birth parents both before and after the placement. Would you like to meet them? Would you prefer to meet them only once at the hospital, or would you be willing to meet them prior to the baby's delivery? Some adopting parents allow their birth mother to stay with them during part of the pregnancy. Is this acceptable to you? In many open adoptions, the birth mother receives a letter and photographs once or twice a year after the baby is placed. Would you agree to this?

. . .

PHIL: *"I was initially uneasy about the openness concept. I was somewhat more willing to speak with the birth mother before we had the baby, but I thought that once the baby was home I wouldn't want any communication with her at all. I was afraid she would harass us, or that the communication would interfere with my ability to bond. But after we connected with our birth mother, a lot of these concerns were put to rest. I realized that she was fairly mature and was also interested in getting on with her life after the placement. The process of getting to know her better helped address a lot of my fears. Now I am fine with the idea of sending pictures and letters once a year. In fact, I look forward to doing it."*

. . .

Adoption Professionals

All legal adoptions must be monitored by either an attorney or adoption agency. Also, some states allow other adoption intermediaries to assist with planning. Chapter 4 will provide information to help you select the best professional team.

Your Budget

The next chapter will provide information on adoption expenses.

Now that you are ready to embrace the concept of adoption, let's begin to address the actual nuts and bolts of the process. As the first practical step, you must establish your personal adoption budget. To do so, you have to gain a realistic understanding of what a private adoption might cost, identify the parameters of your own financial situation, and fashion an adoption budget that will work for you.

Before proceeding to the next chapter, however, be sure you are ready to adopt by reviewing the following points discussed in this chapter:

CHECKLIST FOR CHAPTER 2

- You are emotionally ready to adopt.
- You are prepared to cope with the uncertainty of the adoption process.
- You have begun the necessary homework to learn all you can about adoption.
- You have set up your adoption filing system.

- You have resolved to:
  -participate actively in the adoption process.
  -be realistic and flexible about your expectations.

- You have identified your personal limits and preferences concerning:
  -the characteristics of both child and birth parents.
  -the degree of potential legal risk you are willing to accept.
  -your philosophy on financial assistance and birth parent contact.

3

ॐ

STEP TWO: ESTABLISH
YOUR BUDGET

Although comparable in terms of overall expense, both domestic and international adoptions can vary greatly (between $8,000 and $30,000 for domestic versus $7,000 to $25,000 for intercountry). In some circumstances, expenses can be higher. Couples who have endured years of unsuccessful infertility treatment may not have the financial reserves to attempt adoption. But others may believe incorrectly that they cannot afford adoption or that there is nothing they can do to reduce or to defray expenses. In fact, there are many options for keeping your expenses at reasonable levels. And although financial concerns are a reality for those with infertility, remember that few people who have achieved their dream to adopt will later have regrets over the costs involved.

· · ·

TERI: *"A lot of people express an interest in how much our adoption cost. Many times, it's practically the first question they ask. Maybe they think everyone gets*

(continued on page 63)

FACTORS AFFECTING COST

Because of the many variables at play in any given adoption, it's very difficult to offer specific cost figures. Instead, adoption expenses are usually described in terms of ranges between reported lows and highs. (See table.) Factors that affect the overall cost of an adoption are discussed below.

Length of time between the initial contact with a pregnant woman and her due date. A woman who is not expected to deliver for several months will likely require more in the way of birth mother expenses than one with a more immediate due date.

Medical insurance. If your birth mother is not covered by health insurance, she may be eligible for her state's Medicaid program. (It is estimated that approximately 50 percent of birth mothers qualify for Medicaid.) Every state has programs designed to offer free medical services to women of low income and most states will cover physician and hospital services at no cost. Ask your attorney or other adoption worker to determine if your birth mother is covered or is eligible for coverage. Your own insurance may pay for hospital nursery and pediatrician charges once the baby is born. In fact, the Omnibus Budget Reconciliation Act of 1993 requires group health plans to provide dependent coverage for children placed for adoption from the time most adoptive families assume physical custody of their child. And they must provide insurance coverage of all health expenses in the same way they would for a birth child, including any conditions that existed before placement. This requirement applies whether or not the adoption has become final.

Living expenses. Some birth mothers have little or no need for help with living expenses. However, you may have to search a little harder to find one.

Interstate adoptions. If the child will be born in another state, you will usually need to hire an attorney or adoption agency in that state in addition to your own attorney. This is to ensure the adoption is in compliance with the Interstate Compact on the Placement of Children (ICPC). (See chapter 10 for more details.)

Variations in state statutes. Some states require adoptive parents to pay for separate legal representation for birth parents in addition to their own legal representation. States also vary in what may be considered reasonable financial assistance for birth mothers. If your birth mother lives in a state that restricts assistance, your expenses will be lower.

Birth mother's geographical location. Birth mother living expenses are often influenced by a region's cost of living. Reasonable expenses for such costs as food, housing, and transportation are determined by what is considered appropriate for that area.

Travel. Adopting parents who travel to a different state for the birth of the child must plan for round-trip airfare as well as other related expenses such as hotel and rental car charges.

ADOPTION COSTS

According to the National Adoption Information Clearinghouse, the ranges for domestic adoption costs are as follows:

	LOW	HIGH
Attorney Fees		
Document prep	$500	$2,000
Petition and court representation to finalize placement	$2,500	$12,000
Advertising	$500	$5,000
Birth parent expenses		Amount and type of expenses allowable for

	LOW	HIGH
	payment usually restricted by state law and subject to review by the court.	
Medical expenses	$0 (if insured)	$10,000– $20,000
Living expenses	$5,000	$12,000
Legal representation	$500	$1,500
Counseling	$500	$2,000

If a birth mother is eligible for a Medicaid program, the state pays for the baby's delivery and the adopting parents can eliminate the hospital cost related to the baby's birth.

(continued from page 60)

ripped off. But although our adoption was fairly expensive, I believe the expenses were legitimate and worthwhile. Yes, for what our adoption cost, you could have bought a nice new car. But we didn't want a car. A car is just a car. We now have a family and a future."

. . .

When estimating adoption costs it is essential to keep two points in mind. First, the overall cost of your adoption will frequently be more than you had planned. This is because many expenses simply cannot be anticipated. For example, mother or child may have medical complications or the birth mother may experience an unexpected crisis. Also, once you have committed to a birth mother, it may be very difficult to refuse a request for additional assistance.

This will be especially true just prior to the baby's arrival. So, when it comes to calculating your adoption budget, you must expect—and plan—for the unexpected. The following text provides an overview of normal expenses.

ATTORNEY'S FEES

The total amount spent on legal services will vary between $3,000 and $14,000, depending on the complexity of the case and the attorney's rate. Some attorneys charge by the hour while others have a predetermined flat fee. Many attorneys will require a retainer—a partial up-front payment, which can vary but is usually between $1,000 to $3,000. Once the retainer is exhausted, the attorney will bill you for the balance of the fees as further services are rendered. The following guidelines will help keep your attorney expenses to reasonable levels.

• **Find out what is included in flat fees.** If you are considering an attorney who charges a flat fee, be sure to ask what the fee includes. Determine if the fee includes all legal fees and court costs including court appearances, and travel expenses to and from the courthouse. Birth father's rights termination can involve unique requirements, which may lead to additional fees. Home study fees, and legal, medical, and living expenses for the birth mother are usually not included in an attorney's fees.

• **Consider more than fees or rates when choosing an attorney.** An experienced adoption attorney often charges more than one who is less familiar with adoption issues, but he or she may be more knowledgeable and can work more efficiently than one who does not specialize in adoption.

• **Be cautious about any attorney who requests his entire fee or a very large retainer up front.** This is especially true if the fee is nonrefundable. Most attorneys do not ask for all the adoption fees and expenses up front. Instead, they charge some portion of their fee in advance, and the balance of the fee is usually requested as further services are provided.

• **Be cautious about large initial consultation fees.** If the charge is over $400, ask how many hours this initial session will last. If it's more than a couple of hours, perhaps a larger fee is justified.

• **Ask the attorney to estimate expected legal expenses and ask what can be done to help keep his fees down.** It is not advisable to tell the attorney that you have serious financial concerns, as he may question your ability to adopt and to provide for a child. However, it is certainly appropriate to say that you are trying to plan your budget and would like to know what you can do to help keep expenses to a reasonable level.

• **Ask your attorney for an itemized bill.** You should be able to review specific charges if fees are charged on an hourly basis, or if you are assessed additional charges over a predetermined flat fee. Be sure to read your statement carefully and question it if necessary.

• **Define and limit attorney contact.** Adequate communication between attorney and client is essential, but both clients and attorneys are occasionally guilty of too much contact. For example, one California attorney billed a client $200 per hour after offering unsolicited advice on numerous trivial matters such as giving directions to the hospital. Many issues, which are not strictly legal or which are not technical or complex in nature, can be handled by the attorney's secretary or paralegal assistant and, thus, be charged at a lower hourly rate. By the same token, emotionally involved adoption clients can also be guilty of excessive contact. Many clients call their attorney just to "check in" or to air personal feelings. A better option is to call a trusted friend or family member, or to seek the help of a professional counselor. Also, you can keep an attorney's hours at a minimum by getting involved more directly with the birth mother. Look for opportunities to reduce your reliance on your attorney and his staff by making some arrangements or collecting additional information yourself. For example, some of the things you can do yourself include accompanying your birth mother on a doctor's visit if she lives nearby. If she lives in another state, you may wish to speak with her directly about when and where to meet in person and how frequently to communicate by phone, letter, or e-mail.

• **Ask the attorney what his policy is for a second attempt.** Although everyone hopes for a successful outcome to their adoption attempt, adoptions can sometimes fail despite everyone's best effort. In these cases, it is worth noting that occasionally attorneys do reduce their fees if a client wishes to try again. Some attorneys— although not most—may offer to reduce their fee by as much as fifty percent for a second attempt.

HOME STUDY

Home study fees often vary from one state to another, and can range from $300 to $3,000. In some states, a state adoption office handles the home study, while in others, a private agency will conduct it. In states where private agencies are used, the agency is allowed to set the fee. It can be worthwhile to call around to check on fees, as there are frequently more than a few agencies per state.

OTHER PROFESSIONAL EXPENSES

Identified Agency Fees

An identified adoption is a hybrid form of independent adoption in which a birth mother and adoptive parents locate one another, but then enlist the help of a licensed adoption agency rather than an adoption attorney. This is the only type of independent adoption allowed in four states: Massachusetts, Colorado, Connecticut, and Delaware. The agencies that handle identified adoption usually charge a standard fee of $5,000 to $15,000, which is much less than a standard infant agency adoption. Some agencies include legal fees and birth mother expenses. In other cases, the agency will charge you for these expenses in addition to their basic fees.

Adoption Facilitators

Adoption facilitators, sometimes called consultants, are unlicensed adoption specialists who match birth mothers and adopting couples for a fee. Some will assist in writing and/or placing ads and screening callers. Many feel their job is done once a match has been found, while others will continue to work for you by actively coordinating the many details of the adoption plan. Because of the wide variation in services provided by adoption facilitators, you must be careful to ask what is included for their fee. Fees also vary widely, from $3,000 to $12,000 or more and are no indication of the amount or quality of services provided. An adoption facilitator cannot be substituted for an adoption attorney or agency. Therefore, unless a facilitator charges a very low fee and is actively involved in post-match coordination—offsetting some hourly attorney fees—the use of a facilitator may add significantly to the overall cost of your adoption.

A facilitator should be used only when there is good coordination among you, the facilitator, and your attorney. All three of you should work together in the screening and information-gathering processes and have direct contact with the prospective birth mother and each other. Hopeful parents who wish to keep their overall costs to a minimum, however, can be adequately prepared by using this book as an adjunct to the guidance provided by a capable adoption attorney or an adoption agency.

BIRTH MOTHER EXPENSES

As previously discussed, state laws define the amount and type of expenses allowable for a birth mother's living expenses. To avoid any appearances of "baby buying," the amount paid is usually subject to review by a judge. Your attorney can help you keep these expenses to a reasonable level. In many cases, funds will be placed in your attorney's escrow account. He or she will then disburse small amounts to the birth mother as needed. Keep a careful record of all money paid and don't hesitate to ask for an itemized accounting. View with caution any birth mother who asks for a specific sum of money up front or requests funds for items not directly related to pregnancy. Some women may simply be misinformed about the law while others may intentionally be trying to take advantage. Never send any money directly to a pregnant women without first checking with your attorney or agency.

The types of birth mother expenses you may encounter are:

Medical Expenses

Hospital and medical care for mother and child varies considerably depending on the existence of health insurance coverage and the type of medical care needed. The types of medical charges adopting parents can expect include prenatal, birth and delivery, postnatal care for the mother, and perinatal care for the child. The average cost of a normal pregnancy and delivery of a baby in the United States is between $6,000 and $10,000. If the mother requires a Cesarean section, you can expect an additional $2,000 to $3,000. Although major medical complications can add thousands more, it is estimated that 85 percent of birth mothers will have normal, uncomplicated pregnancies. And of course, as mentioned previously, if the woman has medical insurance coverage, you can expect to pay nothing.

Living Expenses

A birth mother's living expenses can include a few months' rent, utilities, food, clothing, and transportation to the doctor's office. In addition, some birth mothers, particularly those who have undergone a C-section, may require short-term residential maternity care. The total amount of living expenses can vary between $500 and $12,000.

Legal Fees

Some states require separate legal representation for birth mothers. Separate representation is strongly recommended in all cases, and particularly for younger birth mothers. These fees usually vary between $550 and $1,500. Occasionally they may be higher, depending on the involvement required.

Counseling

Some states require that counseling be offered before a woman places a child for adoption. Regardless of the law, counseling should be made available to all birth mothers, even though they may decline it. Counseling fees range from $50 to $125 per hour and can total $500 to $2,000. In some cases, the birth mother's medical insurance may cover these services.

. . .

MIKE: *"We have two adopted children. Our first birth mother was older and was employed. Her employer provided medical insurance. She had a boyfriend who was supportive of the adoption plan. He drove her back and forth to doctor visits and took care of her after the birth. We were asked for very little in the way of pregnancy-related expenses, just a little for clothes. Our second adoption was very different. The girl had only one part-time job and two other kids. No husband or boyfriend. Although she was covered medically, she needed living expenses. We contributed money for her rent, groceries, and clothes. We also had to hire someone to help drive her kids to school for a few weeks after the birth."*

. . .

WAYS TO DEFRAY ADOPTION EXPENSES

Financial assistance is available to families who adopt domestic infants. For example, some companies offer adoption benefits to their employees. Many adopting parents will also be eligible for a tax credit. However, laws concerning tax credits have changed frequently in recent years. At the same time, many IRS agents and accountants may be unfamiliar with the latest information. Therefore it is essential for you, the adopter, to obtain the latest information, which you can get by contacting the Internal Revenue Service or the National Adoption Information Clearinghouse. (See the appendix for further information on all of the entries that follow.)

Federal Adoption Tax Credit

Recent changes in the federal law provide a tax credit for qualified adoption expenses, including adoption fees, court costs, legal fees, and travel expenses including those for meals, rental car, and lodging. In addition, the new law doubles the maximum tax credit from $5,000 to $10,000 and allows for it to be adjusted annually for inflation. As before, the tax credit is progressively phased out for high-income families; however, the new bill increases the income limitations. You can now take the full amount of the credit if your adjusted gross income does not exceed $150,000 (formerly $75,000). This amount decreases as your income approaches $190,000 (formerly $150,000). If you earn above that figure, you will not qualify for the credit.

As an example, if you qualify and owe $10,000 in federal taxes and have $3,000 in qualified adoption expenses, your tax bill is reduced to $7,000. If your tax bill is smaller than the credit, the unused portion of the credit may be carried forward for up to five years. This credit can be claimed even if the adoption is never finalized. For detailed information, be sure to consult with your attorney or tax professional. In addition, you may read or download the law by visiting the legislative service of the Library of Congress at http://thomas.loc.gov. For specific questions, call the Internal Revenue Service at 1-800-829-1040. A summary of current federal tax benefits can also be downloaded from the Web site of the Casey Family Programs National Center for Resource Family Support (see the appendix).

Dependency Exemption

Adoptive parents may take the same dependency exemption on their income taxes for their adopted children as they would for their biological children. This also applies to children who have been placed with adoptive parents prior to the adoption finalization.

Employee Benefits Programs

About a quarter of the nation's employers offer some form of adoption benefits to their employees. These plans offer financial assistance or reimbursement for adoption-related expenses. Assistance varies broadly from one company to another, but amounts usually range from $2,000 to $10,000. Plans may also offer paid leave in addition to or including vacation time, sick leave, or personal days, or unpaid leave, which may range from three to twelve months. Some companies offer a combination of financial help and leave time. As part of their adoption benefits package, a growing number of companies offer their employees adoption seminars and information classes, as well as counseling and support before and after placement. If your expenses exceed what your employer offers, you may combine your employee benefit with the federal tax credit, but you must subtract your employee assistance before applying the tax credit. For example, if your total adoption expenses are $15,000 and your employer gave you $5,000, you must exclude the $5,000 from the federal tax credit, taking only a $10,000 federal income tax credit.

In those companies offering adoption benefits, assistance is typically available to all full-time or regular employees. In some cases, the employee needs to have worked for the company for a specified amount of time, while in others, enrollment in the company's insurance plan is required. Occasionally, companies offer adoption-related benefits not part of a separate adoption benefits plan. Government employees may also qualify for adoption benefits. Ask your employer about adoption benefits even if a plan is currently unavailable. You may be able to persuade your company to begin offering one.

Military Subsidies

The military will reimburse active-duty personnel for most adoption costs up to $2,000 per child for adoptions handled by a nonprofit private or state agency. Travel costs are not covered. The military also provides free health care for adopted children from the time of placement in your home. Contact the Adoption Exchange Association for details.

Once you have a general understanding of the adoption expenses you may anticipate, how do you find all the funds? A few lucky couples may already have everything they need tucked away in the form of savings or investments. But others may have to use some creative strategies to afford their adoption dream. Various methods include applying for a loan, asking family members for help, relying on credit cards, or even dipping into future retirement savings. Low interest or home equity loans can be a good solution, especially for those who are eligible for tax credits or employee benefits and can pay the money back soon. Adoption loans and grants are also available through the National Adoption Foundation, information on how to contact the NAF is provided at the back of the book.

Now that you have a clearer picture of your adoption budget, it's time to assemble your professional team of adoption helpers. But before you do, be sure you are ready to move forward by reviewing the following checklist:

CHECKLIST FOR CHAPTER 3

- You are aware of the various factors affecting adoption costs.
- You understand how to keep attorney fees to a reasonable level.
- You know what to expect with birth mother expenses.
- You know how to defray adoption expenses.
- You have contacted your employer to check on adoption benefits.
- You have contacted your accountant or the IRS for specific questions about adoption tax credit.

4

STEP THREE: ASSEMBLE
YOUR PROFESSIONAL TEAM

As mentioned before, the Fast Track approach is not a do-it-yourself method. Like all adoptions, you must rely on competent experts for advice and guidance along the way. Fortunately, there are a variety of excellent adoption helpers that are available to assist prospective adoptive parents. These include attorneys, agencies, facilitators, and counselors. Would-be parents should recruit a team of adoption professionals, which, at a minimum, will consist of their adoption attorney, the birth parents' attorney, and an adoption counselor. Other helpers may be added according to your needs and preferences. You must not attempt to arrange an adoption without first recruiting competent professional assistance. The ability to make sound decisions rests on proper access to accurate information and qualified professional expertise. Prospective adopters who do not avail themselves of appropriate assistance may participate unwittingly in risky or illegal practices or succumb to unscrupulous profiteers out to defraud them of thousands of dollars. This chapter discusses the professionals you will need and the specific roles they will play in making your adoption dream a reality.

When recruiting your team, it is important to keep in mind that wide variability exists among adoption professionals. Even workers in the same speciality can have significant differences in expertise, training, experience, and philosophy. Be sure to spend some time talking with them, preferably in person, before you agree to work together. In addition to being experienced and knowledgeable, your adoption specialists must also have good "people skills." This is especially important because the experts you hire will also be talking with, and possibly meeting with, the birth parents and their family. As such, they will be your representatives and be a reflection on you. If you don't find them warm and personable, a potential birth mother may not either and may look elsewhere.

. . .

LIZ: *"We had communicated with our birth mother for a couple of months before her due date. In the course of our conversations, she told me that she felt the paralegal in our attorney's office was being insensitive to her. By then, our relationship was pretty solid and I wasn't worried that she would look for another adoptive family. But I did mention something to the attorney about it. After that, all of her calls to the law office were handled directly by the attorney.*

. . .

ADOPTION ATTORNEYS

Your attorney will be the single most essential member of your professional team. A knowledgeable attorney will not only be your legal expert, but he or she will be an invaluable resource for most practical matters as well. Most adoption attorneys will offer advice on advertising, assist in screening birth mother candidates, and coordinate many details of the adoption plan once a match is made. In addition, an adoption attorney can offer valuable advice on other adoption workers and in some cases will assist you in locating them. Therefore, your first step in assembling your professional team is to obtain a competent attorney.

Because the laws governing the adoption process can be complex, it is essential to hire an attorney who specializes in adoption. Do not select an attorney who has a general practice or specializes in another type of law, including family law. Your attorney should be experienced in domestic infant adoption and devote all or a majority of his practice to adoption.

. . .

JANET: *"The first attorney we hired was recommended by several friends as being very inexpensive. He was also located right in our own town, which was very convenient for us. But we were a bit hesitant because he handled other types of law and seemed to do adoptions on the side. Unfortunately, we were right to be concerned. We soon discovered that his knowledge about adoption was very limited. Several months after we met with him, he told us about a birth mother who liked our profile. There appeared to be a lot of potential problems with the case. For example, she knew the whereabouts of the father but had not informed him about her plan to place the baby for adoption. We were concerned about the potential risk, but when we questioned our attorney he kept reassuring us that the father didn't need to be notified immediately. We felt uneasy with this, so we contacted an attorney who only did adoptions. The new attorney agreed that the situation could be very risky. After this, we decided to pass on the first attorney and his birth mother and are now searching for another birth mother under the guidance of our new attorney."*

. . .

It is important to recognize that attorneys, like agencies, often vary in their attitudes toward adoption. When selecting an attorney, explore his attitudes on the issues that are important to you. The attorney you select should have a philosophy that matches your own. In addition, discuss your desire to search actively for a baby and determine his attitude on using adoption advertising to locate a birth mother. This should be established in the initial consultation session. Before hiring an attorney, be sure that he appears willing and able to support or aid your desire to search proactively for your baby.

Determine what your attorney's exact role will be in assisting you. In a few states, attorneys are not permitted to act as an intermediary by bringing prospective birth and adoptive parents together. In these cases, your attorney can handle the legal work and guide you in your efforts to search for a baby but is not allowed to receive calls from potential birth mothers. Therefore, if you are using an attorney who may not act as an intermediary your role will be to place the ads and field the calls. Attorneys who serve as intermediaries can assume a more active role in your effort to search for a baby. For example, they may permit you to include their toll-free telephone number or e-mail address in your ad. Prospective birth mothers would then have the choice of contacting either you or your attorney. (However, most will prefer to speak to you first.)

Keep in mind that some attorneys who serve as intermediaries may offer to locate a birth mother for you. In these cases, the attorney maintains a list of clients waiting to adopt. Those interested in adding their names to the list are asked to provide a copy of their autobiographical profile. Prospective birth mothers are offered a selection of client profiles for consideration. If you find an attorney who maintains a list, you should definitely ask to add your name to it. If you do, think of the attorney's list as simply another "iron in the fire" and continue to focus efforts on your own advertising campaign.

Be certain the attorney you select is experienced and able to assist with all aspects of the adoption process, including birth mother screening, information collection, and review of agency contracts and termination documents. Some attorneys who say they handle adoptions may merely file court documents and appear in court at the final hearing. Look for an attorney who can provide comprehensive services. Once you locate a prospective birth mother, your attorney should interview her and obtain personal and medical background information. He should also assess risk by identifying potential legal and practical difficulties, including the birth parents' level of commitment to an adoption plan. If all parties agree to proceed, he will then coordinate many of the details of the adoption plan, such as verifying the pregnancy, obtaining medical records, ascertaining the whereabouts of the birth father, and dispersing legally permissible birth mother expenses. In order to complete the adoption, he will also ensure that the birth parents' rights are properly terminated, file necessary legal documents, and appear in court when required.

Your attorney should also offer birth parents their own legal representation by a separate attorney. This is to ensure they understand the legal process and the consequences of their actions. Even though the adopting parents pay the fee, the attorney's responsibility is solely to their clients, the birth parents. Most attorneys network with other adoption professionals and are prepared to assist you in locating and arranging legal and counseling services for your birth parents. As a final point, although the attorney you select should practice in your home state, it is not necessary that he or she be located in your immediate area.

Questions to Consider When Selecting an Adoption Attorney

1. Find out if the attorney's adoption philosophy matches your own. Does he favor confidential, traditional adoption or open adoption? Is he willing to adjust to your needs? How does he feel about

adoption advertising? What percentage of his clients uses advertising to locate a birth mother? How will he assist you in your advertising efforts? Will he advise you on placing and writing ads? Will he interview the birth mother for you? Or will he help you do the screening process yourself? Can you include his toll-free number in your ad?

2. Ask the attorney about his experience and involvement in the adoption process. Will the attorney do only the legal work or will he also interact directly with a birth mother. Has he done so in the past? Or, in the case of an identified agency adoption, will he communicate directly with the agency social worker? Will he review agency contracts and documents? Will he verify the pregnancy and obtain background information about the birth parents? Will he assist in ascertaining the whereabouts of the birth father? Will he negotiate and disperse permissible birth mother living expenses? Will he be able to advise you about the legal risks of a given adoption situation? How does he determine whether a birth mother is using drugs? Does he simply interview her or does he require the birth mother to undergo drug testing? Can he obtain HIV testing for birth mother or baby?

3. Ask him what percentage of his practice is devoted to adoptions. How many does he handle annually? How many are independent adoptions? Interstate adoptions? How long has he worked in the field of adoption? Keep in mind that some attorneys may be experienced only in traditional agency or stepparent adoptions.

4. What are the fees and how are they structured? Is the fee hourly or a flat rate? Does the attorney require a retainer in advance? What is the average cost of an adoption? (Refer to chapter 3 for more questions to ask regarding legal expenses.)

5. Don't assume things. Ask for documentation. As Karen Lane suggests, "Don't pay any money to anyone until you get proof of the prospective birth mother's pregnancy. This is not just to prove that she is really pregnant, but also to determine her due date as well. For example, if a birth mother says she will need living money until June but her due date is April, obviously there is a problem."

6. Ask the attorney about his philosophy on birth mother counseling. Does the attorney encourage counseling for birth parents? Will he assist in locating a qualified counselor if requested?

7. Check on the attorney's availability. Can he be reached on weekends and after hours if necessary? If a good birth mother candidate calls you on a Friday evening, you or the pregnant woman may wish to speak with the attorney over the weekend. Will after-hours contact be billed at a higher rate? Is he planning any upcoming vacations? If so, when?

8. Assess the attorney's professionalism. Does he seem efficient and organized? Does the attorney and his staff seem caring and sensitive? Can you imagine a birth mother working comfortably with them?

9. Ask the attorney to explain his procedures and what you can expect in terms of frequency of communication and involvement of other staff members, such as a secretary or paralegal.

10. Ask about the attorney's membership in professional organizations. Many qualified adoption attorneys are members of the American Academy of Adoption Attorneys. (You can verify membership by contacting AAAA directly, see the appendix for contact information.)

11. Ask for references. Obtain names of former clients who have used the attorney and ask them if they would discuss their experience with you. Contact the Better Business Bureau or your State Adoption Unit to see if there are any complaints or investigations about the attorneys you are considering (refer to the appendix for more information). You can also check with your state's bar association. Although they will not recommend any particular attorney, they will advise you if any have been the subject of disciplinary actions. You may also be able to obtain additional information from RESOLVE or other adoptive parent support groups in your area (see the appendix for information).

SHOULD YOU USE AN
ADOPTION AGENCY?

Statistics indicate a growing trend in favor of independent adoption. Today, independent adoption accounts for between one-half and two-thirds of all infant adoptions in this country. Because it generally offers greater control over the entire adoption process, this method appeals to both birth and adoptive parents. Rather than relying on an agency as a go-between, both sets of parents often prefer to talk directly, get to know each other and decide for themselves whether the proposed adoption should proceed. In addition, independent adoption is often preferred as a way to avoid the unnecessary and sometimes illogical requirements occasionally employed by some agencies. Birth parents, in particular, may wish to forego what is often perceived as excessive agency scrutiny and procedures.

Adoptive parents can adopt independently, or they can use an agency. How does one decide? In some cases the decision to involve an agency may be guided by legal necessity. For example, some states do not permit independent adoption, currently Connecticut, Delaware, Minnesota, and Massachusetts. Residents of these states are able to pursue an agency adoption that incorporates most of the advantages of an independent adoption, however, the adoptive and birth parents identify each other directly or with the help of an adoption intermediary and then enlist the help of an agency to arrange for the parental rights to be relinquished. This hybrid form of adoption is called an identified or directed agency adoption. Identified agency adoption is considered an agency adoption; therefore, the laws that govern agency adoption apply. Today, most adoption agencies will handle an identified agency adoption.

Other people may have philosophical reasons for choosing to involve an agency. Agencies are widely believed to offer both birth and adoptive parents the education and counseling they need in order to properly consider and follow through on an adoption plan. Birth mother counseling is frequently included in an agency's fee. Some fear that without agency supervision, birth parents will not be properly advised of their options or will be made promises that will later go unfulfilled. Adoption agencies are not the only providers of adoption counseling services, though. Adoption counseling is available from many private practitioners, such as psychologists, independent social workers, psychiatrists, family therapists, and other trained professionals.

Be sure to consider your options carefully before deciding on the method of adoption that you wish to pursue. Because legal considerations will apply, your attorney can help you weigh the pros and cons. If you decide to involve an agency, you should still retain an attorney.

How to Select an Adoption Agency

1. Determine the agency's focus on infant adoption by asking them how many children they placed in the last year and what percentage of them were newborns.

2. Determine the agency's philosophy on identified adoption. Ask if they have an identified adoption program and how long it has been in effect. How many identified placements have they made in the last year? Is the agency's philosophy compatible with your own? Adoption agencies, like adoption attorneys, often adhere to different philosophies about adoption. Inform the agency that you will be actively searching for a birth mother. (Some agencies will offer to assist by adding your name to a list or a pool. If so, you may wish to combine your efforts together with those of the agency's. Others may be biased against identified adoptions, in which case you'll want to look elsewhere.) Determine the agency's philosophy about communication and coordination during the preplacement phase of the adoption. Will they encourage preplacement communication between you and your birth mother? Will they coordinate closely with you and the birth mother? Finally, determine the agency's policy regarding foster care following the delivery. Some states will not permit a baby to be placed in an adoptive home until a certain amount of time has elapsed. This is to allow a birth mother sufficient time to consider her decision to place the child for adoption. In these states, an agency may either require that the child be placed in a foster home or designate the adoptive parents as foster parents and allow the child to go home with the adoptive family. Both sets of parents frequently will not want the child to be placed in a foster home, preferring instead that the child go home directly with the adoptive parents.

3. Ask about the types of services the agency provides for birth mothers. If counseling is offered, a qualified counselor should conduct it face-to-face. Ask the agency about their techniques for determining a birth mother's commitment to an adoption plan. If the agency senses any doubts, will you be notified?

4. Ask the agency for a written fee schedule. Check their fees for various services, including any additional costs for services provided by other professionals. Ask when the fees are due. Most legitimate agencies do not request large amounts of money up front. Typically, services are paid for as they are rendered, with the largest sum collected at or just before the baby's placement. When an agency finds a baby for someone, the fee is usually more than for an identified adoption. Check to see that you are being quoted the fee for an identified adoption. Ask if it includes charges for birth mother's medical and living expenses, home study, and post-placement supervisory visits. Determine whether you will be responsible for birth mother medical expenses in the event that she is uninsured and ineligible for Medicaid. Ask for a written copy of the agency's policy on refunds. Some agencies have a payment plan, and once payment is made the money is not refunded, while others state that a certain portion can be refunded. If the money has already been paid out to another source, such as an adoption counselor or attorney, most agencies will not refund this money. However, some will pay out of their own pockets in order to satisfy the client.

5. Determine if legal services are included in the agency's fees. Some agencies have an attorney on staff who prepares and files legal documents required to complete an adoption. Others will expect you to retain an attorney at your own expense.

6. Check references. Call people who have adopted children through the agency to discuss their experience. Contact the Better Business Bureau for reliability reports on the agency. Also contact your state adoption specialist or the Department of Social Services to check for any complaints or investigations (see the appendix).

7. Finally, ask your attorney to review the agency's contract before signing anything.

WHAT YOU NEED TO KNOW ABOUT ADOPTION FACILITATORS

As independent adoption has become more popular, a new type of adoption helper has emerged. The adoption facilitator, sometimes called adoption consultant, is an unlicensed intermediary whose primary job is to help people find birth mothers for a fee. Facilitators are often adoptive parents themselves who would like to help others by sharing their knowledge and experience. Unfortunately, the level of expertise among facilitators varies dramatically. Unlike lawyers and adoption agencies, adoption facilitators are unlicensed. Consequently, they have no requirements for training and competency and consumers have nowhere to go to file complaints when abuses occur.

Before hiring a facilitator, carefully consider the role he or she will play in your plan to adopt. For example, some excellent facilitators will work closely with you and your attorney to provide extra assistance not only in locating and screening birth mothers but in coordinating post-match adoption details as well. If you can identify one who will provide these services for a reasonable fee, then he or she could be a valuable addition to the team. Remember that you can often receive the same services from many qualified attorneys and agencies without incurring the additional expense of a facilitator. Should you decide to hire a facilitator, consider the following guidelines:

1. A facilitator should be viewed as an adjunct to your core professional team, consisting of you and your attorney (and your agency in the case of an identified agency adoption). One should never be used as a substitute for an attorney or licensed adoption agency.

2. When used, a facilitator should coordinate closely with you and your attorney. You and all the members of your team should communicate frequently to ensure that everyone is equally informed and updated as developments unfold.

3. Do not rely on a facilitator as your only means of locating a birth mother. Many facilitators are poorly equipped to recognize potential red flags, particularly legal ones, and are therefore unable to anticipate difficulties before they occur. As Karen Lane puts it, for some facilitators "matched is matched." Furthermore, much of the hard work in an adoption comes after the birth parents are located. Since they are often paid for the match, a couple can pay a facilitator's full fee before legal problems surface.

4. Seek guidance from your attorney before you hire a facilitator. Facilitators are illegal in several states. In these states, an adoption may not be processed if the child was found through any intermediary not licensed as an adoption agency.

. . .

KATIE: *"We had a bad experience with a facilitator in California. The birth mother she matched us with later changed her mind about placing the baby for adoption and decided to parent the child herself. Looking back on it, I don't believe that the girl was really committed. At the time, we assumed that the facilitator would do a proper job of screening birth mothers. But now I think she just accepts any girl who has even a passing interest in adoption. The facilitator's literature stated that she would work to find us another match if one fell through, but in fact this never happened. We never heard from her again. Of course, we had already paid her full fee. Months later I looked up her Web site and saw that we were listed as one of her success stories. That was the final insult."*

. . .

Questions to Consider Before Hiring a Facilitator

1. What is the facilitator's credentials and experience? Some facilitators are licensed social workers or psychologists, while many lack specific training but have personally experienced the adoption process and would like to assist others. Do they have any special training? Are they a member of any professional organizations? How long have they worked as a facilitator and how many adoptions do they handle each year?

2. What types of services do they offer? Some facilitators will offer to locate a birth mother for you while others will help you search on your own. What role will they play in your adoption? Will they help you screen birth mothers? Will they help with post-match adoption planning? If so, determine which details they will help arrange.

3. How does the facilitator feel about working closely with you and your attorney? Will the three of you be able to coordinate cohesively?

4. What are their fees? Some facilitators charge a flat fee while others charge by the hour. What services are not included?

5. Are they available on weekends and after hours? If you plan to use a facilitator, make sure either your attorney or your facilitator will be available by phone on the weekends while your ads are in place. Check her vacation schedule before placing ads. Will prospective birth parents be speaking with the facilitator or with one of her staff?

6. Ask for references and contact former clients to discuss their experience. Contact your state adoption specialist to see if there have been any complaints (see the appendix). Ask your local adoptive parent support groups for any information or referrals they may have.

7. Consult with your attorney before you pay a facilitator. Is it legal to use a facilitator in your state? How does your attorney feel about coordinating with a facilitator? Can he personally recommend one? If the facilitator has a contract, ask your attorney to review it before signing.

ADOPTION COUNSELORS

Adoption counseling can provide valuable benefits for both sets of prospective parents. Some states, and all adoption agencies, require birth parents to receive or be offered counseling. As stated previously, counseling should be made available to all birth mothers even though they may decline it. Although a birth mother may not at first desire counseling, she may feel differently later on. Birth mothers often report feeling isolated during their pregnancy. For them, counseling provides a much needed support system to help them cope with the range of emotions they will experience both before and after the baby is born. If a pregnant woman has any doubts about her decision, counseling can help identify and resolve these feelings before adopting parents have invested increasing amounts of time, money, and emotions. Following the baby's arrival, the counselor can help her cope with sadness and grief and offer assistance as she moves forward in her life.

Counseling is also available for adopting parents who would like to explore infertility issues and receive support throughout the emotional ups and downs of the adoption process. A qualified mental health professional can assist with decision making and communication skills. Hopeful parents—particularly those who have recently moved from infertility treatments to adoption—may experience sadness, anger, and frustration over the loss of their fertility and the inability to nurture a child from conception. It is not uncommon for adopting parents to have acute fears and anxieties over the eventual outcome of their adoption effort, which has no doubt required considerable sacrifice and commitment on their part. While adopting parents often need emotional support and guidance, few people other than professional counselors are in a position to help. Therefore, when the emotional side of adoption requires attention, prospective adopters would be wise to seek the services of a qualified adoption counselor.

How to Select an Adoption Counselor

Counselors should be selected with care. Although counselors specializing in adoption issues may not be available in every community, it is helpful to find one with some experience in adoption. Above all, they must be unbiased in their approach. This is particularly true if a counselor will be meeting with a prospective birth parent.

Recommendations can be obtained from adoption attorneys, agency social workers, and state or local mental health associations. Local adoptive parents' support groups, such as those organized by RESOLVE or Adoptive Families of America, can also be a good source for referrals. In addition, national professional organizations will provide information on therapists that specialize or have experience in adoption issues in your area (see the appendix).

Many counseling professionals offer a free fifteen- or twenty-minute initial consultation. Take advantage of this opportunity to ask the following questions:

• What is your experience with adoption in general, infertility issues, open adoption, adoptive children, and adoptive families? How long have you been in practice? What degrees, licenses, or certifications do you have? Do you have any special training in adoption issues? What professional organizations are you a member of?

• If the counselor will be meeting with birth parents, ask about his experience with birth parents. Assess the counselor's ability to handle certain issues by asking specific "what if" style questions. For example, you may ask, "If the birth mother has other children, what would you advise her to tell them?" "If the birth mother's mother is having difficulty accepting her daughter's decision, how would you handle this?" "How would you proceed if you suspected that a birth mother was being pressured into her decision by the baby's father?"

• What are your fees? Do you have a policy for missed or late appointments? Do you accept insurance?

• What arrangements do you have for counseling coverage in the event that you are unavailable?

HOW TO AVOID ADOPTION FRAUD

Those seeking to adopt are often aware that illegal or unethical practices occasionally occur in the field of adoption. (However, adoptive parents may not realize that they are not the only potential victims of adoption fraud. When adoptive parents or adoption, workers misrepresent themselves, birth parents can fall prey as well.) Some are so desperate to adopt that they fail to look before they leap. Others are uninformed or feel overwhelmed at the prospect of doing the necessary homework. Attracted by the prospect of instant gratification, some couples fail to question the qualifications and methods of those who promise a baby, often for large up-front fees. Many are tempted to simply hand the money over. Unfortunately, this is a recipe for disaster. Victims of adoption scams report paying up to $25,000, only to wait years to discover there is no baby and no way to recover their money. While most adoption professionals are qualified and act in accordance with legal and ethical practices, some do not.

Therefore, it is essential to select your helpers with care. Observe the following guidelines before you commit to any adoption professional:

1. Never pay any adoption specialist a large up-front fee. Some agencies, attorneys, or facilitators may accept excessive fees from several hopeful clients while actually having few, if any, birth mother prospects. Others may simply "take the money and run."

2. Select only professionals with verifiable contact information. Avoid those who make themselves untraceable by using toll-free

telephone numbers, post office boxes, or e-mail addresses, or who request money wired directly to a bank account. Be cautious of adoption specialists who contact you through the Internet. Some users of Internet chat rooms report being contacted by individuals representing themselves as facilitators. The "facilitator" may claim they know of a birth mother who wishes to place their baby for adoption but requires immediate living expenses before proceeding. Beware. While the Internet can be an important resource for prospective parents, its anonymity also provides a convenient haven for unscrupulous individuals seeking to defraud unwary couples.

3. Obtain detailed answers to your questions. Avoid any adoption specialist who gives evasive answers or provides few details about their qualification and methods.

4. Be suspicious of any adoption arranger who guarantees a baby within a certain amount of time. Most ethical professionals will not make such claims. Also, avoid anyone who pressures you by suggesting that if you do not act quickly by sending money, you will lose an important opportunity.

5. Resolve to be involved in the process from start to finish. Coordinate closely with those you have chosen to assist you. Above all, avoid the temptation to "turn everything over" to an adoption professional and wait for the phone to ring with the happy news. If you do, the financial and emotional cost may simply be too high.

Now that you have assembled your professional adoption team, it is time to arrange for a successful home study. But before proceeding, be sure you have completed the following key points in this chapter.

CHECKLIST FOR CHAPTER 4

- You have interviewed and selected an experienced full-service adoption attorney.
- You have decided whether to recruit the services of an adoption agency or facilitator.
- You have selected an adoption counselor.
- You know how to avoid adoption fraud.

5

Step Four: Obtain an
Approved Home Study

O nce you have assembled your professional team, the next
step is to obtain an approved home study. Unfortunately,
many people misunderstand the purpose of the home
study, and as a result may approach it fearfully. There is nothing to
fear. The purpose of the home study is not to inspect your house
for dust, but to prepare people for their new role as adoptive parents
and to ensure that children placed through adoption will receive
proper care. Required in most states, the home study process is
informative rather than investigative. The social worker, or case-
worker, who conducts your home study is not searching for ways to
eliminate you as an applicant. Most social workers who conduct
home studies are pro-adoption and are eager to help applicants
become adoptive parents. He or she is likely to become an important ally, guiding you toward greater awareness about issues you
might expect as a future adoptive parent. Some questions may be
posed, not to pass judgment, but to stimulate further thought or
discussion. You will not always be expected to know all the answers.

In addition, your social worker may provide further educational opportunities by informing you of support groups and other community resources. You may be encouraged to read books on adoption and childcare or to attend parenting classes with other prospective adoptive parents. Participation in these activities is designed to help you prepare for adoptive parenthood. Complying with the requirements of a home study is often easier once applicants understand that its purpose is to serve the best interests of both you and your future child.

Although some states may not require a home study until after the baby is placed in your home, it is strongly recommended that you undergo your home study before your ads are placed, so that you will be prepared to act fast if needed. In addition, completing it beforehand will also allow you to focus more completely on locating and developing a relationship with your birth mother. You will appreciate having completed this step when it is time to field calls and to learn more about your prospective birth mother. Birth mothers also feel more secure about adopting families who already have met the requirements of a home study. It will be to your advantage to state in your profile or Web site that you have a currently approved home study.

Completing your home study before placing your ad is important for practical and legal considerations, but the best reason is because it will help you thoroughly think through your plans before you commit to adoptive parenting. Parenting an adopted child is not the same as parenting a biological one. Different issues and challenges apply. The home study process, although not perfect, is designed to educate prospective adoptive parents about the realities and demands of the road ahead.

Since each state has its own laws regulating home studies, the exact process, the contents of the written report, and the time it takes for completion will vary from state to state. Your attorney can advise you on the requirements of your specific state. Home studies can be performed by either licensed adoption agencies or authorized social workers. For independent adoptions, they are usually performed by a certified social worker in private practice. Most states also require post-placement supervisory visits designed to monitor the child's progress and your family's adjustment to the placement. Although some variations exist, most home studies elicit applicants' information through documents and one or more personal interviews, including a home visit. Most home studies include the following common elements.

DOCUMENTS

As part of the home study, you will need to provide your social worker with financial and personal information. Your social worker or agency will provide you with the necessary forms to complete as well as a list of other documents, which you will need to supply. You can greatly expedite the process by getting to work now on filling out forms, scheduling your medical appointments, and gathering the necessary documents. The specific documents required may be determined by state law, but will usually include the following:

Birth Certificates, Marriage Certificate, and Divorce Decree if Applicable

State laws do not specifically address the age of the adoption applicant. However, prospective parents over the age of fifty can expect the social worker to focus on health issues and to ask questions to determine your commitment and physical stamina. Applicants who are single, unmarried, or newly married will not be disqualified from becoming adoptive parents. You will also be permitted to adopt if you are divorced. However, because one of the goals of the home study is to assess the stability of the family, you may expect additional questions if you have been divorced multiple times. Most state laws also do not address whether gays may or may not adopt, although a few, currently including Florida and New Hampshire, specifically ban homosexuals from adopting children. Many social workers will not ask your sexual orientation. Gay applicants may choose to not to reveal this information unless specifically asked. If asked, they may choose to withhold this information or decline to answer.

Health Statement

You will be asked to supply a statement, signed by your physician, that describes your general physical and emotional health. This may require a physical exam or a current tuberculosis test. Some medical tests may have to be performed, including those for hepatitis or HIV. The purpose of this statement is to ensure that applicants are essentially healthy, can meet the physical challenges of raising a child, and will have a normal life expectancy. You are not expected to be a specimen of perfect health. People with a variety of conditions or impairments have been approved as adoptive parents. While you will not usually be disqualified for having a condition that can be controlled through supervised medical treatment, a serious health problem that will affect your life expectancy may prevent approval.

People with physical disabilities are often successful in adopting children. A social worker may wish, however, to discuss the severity of your disability, your ability to manage it, and how you plan to keep up with your future child. Therefore, those with disabilities should be prepared to demonstrate their independence by discussing strategies for handling emergency situations as well as practical tasks such as carrying, feeding, and changing a baby.

Most people who have received counseling or medications for emotional problems will also be approved as adoptive parents. In determining eligibility, the social worker will consider the type and severity of the problem, when it occurred, its current status, and the likelihood of future reoccurrence. Social workers also find it acceptable if applicants have received individual or couples counseling to address brief transitory problems (for example, depression following a personal setback or grief from the loss of a loved one).

In addition, prospective adoptive parents often seek help for stress and depression associated with their infertility. Very few social workers would object to applicants who have received help for these concerns. In fact, many will look favorably on applicants who have taken appropriate steps to improve their lives.

Psychiatric conditions that will likely pose a problem include psychosis and any current disorder which is potentially life-threatening, such as severe forms of depression and anorexia. People with a psychosis are out of touch with reality and often require hospitalization. Schizophrenia, bipolar disorder (manic depression), and multiple personality disorder are examples of chronic acute disorders that can reoccur in the future. Therefore, people with these conditions are likely to be disqualified as adoption applicants.

Many social workers will require you to sign a statement declaring that you are not addicted to drugs or alcohol and that you have never received drug or alcohol treatment. If you have received treatment for substance abuse, it is wise to tell your social worker. Usually this information will not disqualify you, but your social worker will wish to obtain more information to be satisfied that the problem is resolved and the risk of reoccurrence is minimal.

Income Statement

The purpose of the income statement is to determine your general financial stability. You will be asked to verify your income by providing copies of recent income tax statements or paycheck stubs. You will also be asked about your savings, health and life insurance policies, investments, and debts, including your mortgage, car, or rent payments. The social worker will not expect you to be wealthy, but you should be able to demonstrate your ability to manage your finances responsibly. In addition, you must show that you have enough money saved to handle emergencies and to meet the needs of a child.

Police and Child Abuse Clearance

Most states require adoption applicants to undergo criminal record and child abuse record clearances. You will usually be provided with forms requiring you to complete identifying information such as your name, date of birth, and Social Security number. You will then submit them to your state child welfare agency and local or state police department. Authorities will check to see if you have any known criminal or child abuse charges on file. Some states may require you to obtain an FBI clearance. If so, you may be asked to be fingerprinted. Minor offenses, such as traffic violations or an isolated shoplifting charge committed years ago are usually not sufficient to disqualify you. A social worker is unlikely to recommend you as an adoptive parent, however, if you or anyone living in your home has committed a felony or have been convicted of child abuse or neglect. All adults living in your home will be asked to undergo the same criminal and child abuse screening as you.

Personal References

You will be asked to provide the names, addresses, and telephone numbers of several individuals who will serve as references for you. Most social workers require between three and five references from individuals other than family members. References are used to establish your character and ability to build healthy relationships, and to determine if others perceive you as a good candidate for parenthood. Carefully consider your choices for references.

Although your application is unlikely to be rejected on the basis of one negative reference, it may unnecessarily complicate the process. Do not list anyone's name before checking with the person first. Be sure they understand the importance of what you are asking of them.

PERSONAL INTERVIEWS

You can expect one or more personal interviews, including one visit in which a social worker will come to your home. The social worker may hold other interviews in the office and may meet with you and your spouse separately or together. These interviews will center on the following aspects:

- Motivation to Adopt
- Autobiographical Information
- Marriage
- Parenting Attitudes and Values
- Adoption Issues
- House and Community

Questions You May Be Asked

While the exact questions will vary from one home study to the next, the following are a sample of those you might expect:

Autobiographical Information
- Where were you born and raised?
- How many siblings do you have? Describe their age(s), sex, occupation(s), and health. Where do they currently live? What is your current relationship with them?

- If your parents are still living, what are their ages? What are their occupations? Where do they currently reside?
- What is your relationship with your parents, both now and in the past?
- What values did your parents emphasize?
- Where did you attend school?
- What degrees or diplomas did you earn?
- Was education (or sports, etc.) emphasized in your home as a child?
- What types of extracurricular activities did you participate in as a child?
- What types of activities did you participate in with your family?
- What method of discipline was used in your home as a child?
- What are your current hobbies and interests?
- Which past achievements, both personal and occupational, are you most satisfied with and why?
- What is your current and past work history?
- What are your long-term employment goals?
- Do you plan to continue working after the arrival of your child?
- Does your job require you to travel?
- What is the length of leave time you can obtain immediately following placement of your child?
- How will you handle child-care arrangements if you must return to work? Do you have other children? If so, what are their ages?
- If you have children from a previous marriage, do they live with you? If not, how often you see them? What types of activities do you enjoy together?

- How will your other children be affected by the addition of an adopted child?

Your Marriage*

- When and how did you meet your spouse?
- What attracted you to your spouse?
- When were you engaged?
- Have either of you been married before? If so, what difficulties did you encounter in previous marriages?
- Have you ever sought marriage counseling?
- How would you describe your spouse and your marriage?
- What do you most admire about your spouse?
- What interests and activities do you share in common?
- How do you make decisions and resolve conflict?
- How do you divide household tasks?
- How do you intend to handle child-care responsibilities?
- How has your relationship changed over the years?
- How would you like it to grow in the future?
- How will a child change your lifestyle and marriage?

*If you are single

- Describe your current close relationships and any past marriages, if any.
- Are you seeing anyone who may become closely involved with your child?
- How do you feel about marrying in the future?
- What are your plans for child care if you should become sick and cannot care for your child?
- Are there any close relatives or friends that could be counted on in an emergency?

Infertility and Adoption Issues

- If infertile, what is your medical diagnosis? How long have you known you are infertile?
- Have you undergone infertility treatments or consulted with an infertility specialist? Will you be continuing infertility treatments in the future?
- What impact has your infertility had on your marriage and other family members?
- How did you shift your focus from pregnancy to adoption?
- Why are you pursuing adoption now?
- Do you feel you can bond with a child that is not genetically related to you?
- How will parenting an adopted child differ from parenting a biological one?
- Do you think your child should be told about being adopted? If so, how and when do you intend to talk with your child about his beginnings?
- How will you handle other people's questions about adoption?
- What are your attitudes toward birth parents?
- How much contact would you like with your child's birth parents, both before and after placement?
- How do you feel about the possibility that your child may later wish to meet his birth parents?
- What is the age, ethnicity, and health of the child you seek to adopt?
- If you adopt a child of a different race or ethnicity, what are your views about people of that background? How do other members of your family feel about a child of a different heritage? How will you handle questions from others if your child does not look like you? Will you seek out members of the same race for your child to identify with?

- How flexible can you be about a child's race and health?
- Are you currently in touch with a prospective birth mother? If so, describe your relationship and frequency of contact.
- Are you pursuing an independent or identified agency adoption?
- What resources are you using for adoption support and education?
- Would you like to learn of additional resources?

Parenting Issues and Values

- Why do you wish to become a parent?
- What qualities do you and your spouse have that will allow you to be suitable parents?
- What is your past and current experience with children? Have you ever, or do you currently, baby-sit for friends or siblings? Have you ever worked with children? Are you, or have you ever been, involved in any children's organizations?
- How do you intend to acquire additional parenting skills?
- Would you like to learn about additional parenting resources?
- What method of discipline do you intend to use? How will this differ from the one used by your parents?
- What attitudes and values do you hope to pass on to your child?
- What goals would you like to see your child achieve?
- What is your religious background and current practices? Are they the same as your spouse? If not, how do you intend to raise your child?
- If you do not participate in religious activities, how do you intend to encourage strong family values?

Your Home

- If you own your home, what did you pay for it and what is its current value? What is your equity or the monetary value of the property beyond any amounts owed on it in the form of mortgages, claims, or liens? And what is your mortgage payment?
- Do you expect to be making any major changes to your home or current living arrangements?
- Do you anticipate moving in the near future?
- Why did you select this neighborhood?
- Can you describe the community resources in your area—schools, medical facilities, parks, libraries, museums, and so on?
- Do you know and like your neighbors? What kind of people are they?
- What are the safety features of your property and neighborhood?

Finances

- What is your combined income?
- What are your assets and liabilities?
- What are your savings and investments?
- What types of insurance do you have (medical, disability, life)?
- Will your medical insurance cover an adopted child?
- Do you have a pension or retirement plan?

A sample home study is provided in the appendix.

How to Prepare for a Home Study Interview

Most people are understandably nervous at the prospect of being evaluated, especially when central issues of their future are at stake. Remember that the purpose of the interview process is not simply to assess you, but also to offer education and support as well. The vast majority of social workers conducting home studies are eager to provide any help they can and are receptive to your questions about adoption issues and community resources. Many are also adoptive parents themselves and appreciate the challenges you are experiencing. By viewing the interviews as an opportunity to connect with your social worker and to add to your growing understanding of the adoption process, you will be better prepared for a successful experience.

As noted, a key objective of the home study process is to help prospective parents adjust to adoptive parenthood. Use the days and weeks prior to your home study to reflect on your feelings about parenting and adoption issues. If married, talk with your partner about these issues before the interviews take place. Each partner must have the chance to discuss his or her feelings openly and honestly. Try to identify attitudes and experiences you share in common, as well as those on which you differ. Do you expect that your parenting styles will be the same, or could they complement each other? If so, how? Identify any special qualities that could make you and your spouse a good parent.

Although very few personal problems will disqualify you as adoption applicants, you should identify and prepare for sensitive subjects. As noted, most applicants will obtain an approved home study unless they have committed a felony, been convicted of child abuse (or live with someone convicted of child abuse), have a severe psychiatric disorder, have a life-threatening medical condition, or are currently in treatment for substance abuse. For other problems such as chronic health problems, multiple divorces, a difficult childhood, or past histories of minor arrests or drug or alcohol use, it is best if you do additional preparation in advance.

Talk with your attorney about your areas of concern and get his or her advice. He may be aware of an agency or social worker who may be sympathetic to your situation. If you think you or someone you live with may have been investigated for a criminal offense, your attorney can contact the appropriate agency to see if there is anything on record. Be prepared to answer questions about the problem during the home study interview. Although you are not required to disclose every difficult situation, always answer honestly if the social worker asks a direct question or notices something of concern in your records. Where possible, try to identify the positive aspects of the situation. For example, if you have a previous arrest involving drugs or alcohol, you should be prepared to demonstrate how you sought assistance or otherwise dealt successfully with your problem.

If you have a chronic medical condition, it may help to provide a statement from your doctor explaining that your condition is stable, will not affect your longevity, and is easily controlled with proper medical supervision. Reassure the social worker that your medical condition will not affect your ability to keep up with an active child—if this is indeed true. If you were abused as a child (neglect, physical, emotional, or sexual) and the social worker asks about the presence of child abuse in your past, you must answer honestly. But be prepared to discuss how it has affected you, the resources you used to cope, and the ongoing measures you intend to take to safeguard your children from experiencing similar abuse. Keep in mind that the social worker will not expect you to be perfect in all ways.

How to Prepare for the Home Study Visit

One way to get ready for the home study visit is to prepare other people who may live in your home. If you already have children at home, they will most likely be present at one or more of the interviews. Many social workers will have a few questions for them to determine their feelings about a proposed addition to the family. Also, because the safety of your future child is so important, this is a good time to take an objective look at your pets to consider their compatibility with small children. For example, if you have a particularly large dog that rules the house, now may be the perfect time to install that outdoor dog run. Although the social worker will not scrutinize your pets, they should appear clean, friendly, and well cared for. Inspect your house and yard for safety concerns and make necessary repairs or develop appropriate plans in advance of the visit. For example, you may wish to protect stairs, or formulate a plan to childproof them when the time comes. Ensure you have adequate smoke detectors and at least one wall-mounted fire extinguisher located in a convenient place. Lock up your firearms if you have them, and devise a plan for safeguarding medicines, and house and garden chemicals. If you have a swimming pool, plan on having it fenced, if it isn't already.

Other points to remember:

- Always answer questions honestly. As noted, you are not obliged to volunteer past indiscretions, but you must be honest if asked directly. Remember to discuss how you were able to resolve the difficulty, if this is in fact the case.
- It is appropriate to offer the social worker a simple beverage, but you do not have to go overboard with fancy snacks.

- Clear a table in advance, perhaps the dining room table, where you can all sit together. The social worker will appreciate having a suitable place to take notes.
- If your pet is the energetic type, find an out-of-the-way spot for him while the visit takes place. Even animal lovers can be uncomfortable if greeted by a dog's excessive jumping or barking.
- If your house is hard to find, and the social worker is unfamiliar with your area, provide him in advance with good directions.

To be sure you are fully prepared for your home study, view the sample home study report provided in the appendix. Once you understand what to expect and your home study is scheduled, it is time to prepare an effective profile. But before continuing, review the following points to be certain you are ready to proceed.

CHECKLIST FOR CHAPTER 5

- You understand the purpose of a home study.
- You have selected the agency or adoption worker who will perform your home study.
- You have requested the necessary forms and documents you must submit.
- You are in the process of scheduling medical appointments and gathering or completing the necessary documents.
- You know what questions to expect during a home study interview.

6

STEP FIVE: PREPARE AN EFFECTIVE PROFILE

Once your home study is under way, your next task will be to write your autobiographical profile. The profile is commonly described by many different names, including resume, portfolio, or Dear Birth Mother Letter. However, for the sake of simplicity, this book will refer to all of these variations as profile. An essential part of open adoptions for years, profiles traditionally use words and pictures to provide a description of who you are.

Intermediaries such as adoption agencies and attorneys typically ask their clients to provide profiles so that a potential birth mother can learn about waiting families and possibly select one for her child. However, adopting parents who plan to advertise for a birth mother should also create a profile. Why? Even though you will have an opportunity to speak personally with callers, your profile will provide them with an additional, more tangible source of information. As a supplement to your telephone or on-line exchanges, it will further assist her in forming a picture of who you are, what your lives are like and the type of future you can offer a child. After your baby is home, the profile can also be a wonderful keepsake for both you and your birth mother. Since it may take up to a month to complete, it's a good idea to start work on yours at your earliest opportunity.

There is no single way to construct a profile. You have the freedom to design your profile in the way that best showcases your own unique features and personality. Profiles vary considerably in their length, look, and format. Some are straightforward and serious, while others are whimsical or humorous. In addition, many hopeful parents choose to illustrate their message with artwork or anecdotes. Length also varies considerably. Some profiles consist of one page and include only one photograph, others range fifteen or more pages with numerous photos. In addition, there are any number of things you may choose to describe, including the life you see for your child, your home, background, religion, marriage, family, and hobbies. Regardless of its form and contents, your profile should provide a unique and authentic reflection of you.

Because your goal is to allow your own personality to shine through, most of the following guidelines are offered tentatively. Feel free to reject these suggestions if the best way to reveal yourself is to create your own set of rules.

In most cases, your autobiographical profile will be one of your first experiences in communicating with a birth mother. If properly executed, it will lead to many more opportunities to communicate with the woman who may ultimately become your child's birth mother. Consequently, your profile should be viewed as the first step in building a strong and lasting relationship with your birth mother. Also, although they are presented now, these same rules apply for all aspects of communicating with a birth mother, both now and in the future, including placing ads and responding to calls, as well as any interaction both before and after your child's homecoming. By applying these rules now, you will be developing good communication habits that will serve you well in the future.

Be honest. Many prospective adoptive parents fear the "beauty contest" aspect of having to be evaluated and selected by a pregnant woman. They believe they will not be chosen unless they appear "perfect." But this is untrue. Birth mothers frequently share many of the same qualities that you perceive as weaknesses. Many birth mothers are single, rent apartments, or live in modest-sized homes. Often they will relate easily to other people who share similar characteristics. Furthermore, the fact that a birth mother will be choosing you can be an advantage. Birth mothers often evaluate prospective families differently than adoption agencies do.

Therefore, when describing yourselves to birth parents, it is far more important to be honest than to appear "perfect." In fact, the old adage "honesty is the best policy" is vitally important with respect to all forms of communication with birth parents, including the text and visual images of your profile. Birth mothers considering a home for their child often wonder if things really are as they appear to be. It is your responsibility to strive for authenticity in both the words and pictures you present. Avoid retouched or digitally altered photos. Do not misrepresent yourself in an effort to become more appealing to a birth mother. Adoptions based on illusions and false promises violate a sacred trust and can unravel fast. Also, keep in mind that you are not trying to connect with every birth mother. You are trying to connect with the one that's right for you.

Be positive. Because your autobiographical profile will provide a birth mother with one of the first glimpses of who you are, it should highlight the very best qualities that you bring to your future role as adoptive parents. Many birth mothers will only view your profile once before forming an opinion. In some cases, the facts that you perceive as relative weaknesses can be presented honestly but stated in positive terms. For example, if you fear you may be rejected because you live in a large city, you might emphasize the benefits of city life, such as close proximity to excellent parks, schools, medical facilities, and museums.

Once your profile has attracted a birth mother's attention, follow-up conversations will provide her with the opportunity to get to know you better and to ask about anything of concern. Adopting parents commonly have many doubts, fears, and feelings of inadequacy. Avoid dwelling on your infertility or any other losses experienced in your life. Birth mothers are aware that many adopting parents have experienced the sadness of infertility, but the reality is that they would prefer to focus on resolving their own current difficulties. Show a prospective birth mother that you are excited and happy at the prospect of becoming parents through adoption. Design your profile to inspire and encourage.

Be respectful. Pregnant women who consider adoption plans for their babies deserve to be treated with respect. Prospective birth mothers must draw on their strength and courage to decipher a confusing process, overcome numerous hurdles, make difficult choices, and endure considerable physical and emotional discomfort. And they often do so alone, without the support of a partner, friends, or family. Of all the parties involved in an adoption, the birth mother makes the greatest sacrifice. Therefore, it is never appropriate to speak to a birth mother using a condescending or judgmental tone.

It would also be a serious mistake to assume that all birth mothers are uneducated and from a poor background. Many different types of women experience unwanted pregnancies, and personal characteristics of birth mothers vary broadly. Fortunately, unplanned pregnancies do not carry the stigma that they used to. Still, birth mothers often feel embarrassment and humiliation over being unable or unwilling to care for their child. Most birth mothers will appreciate any efforts you make to reach out to her in a genuine spirit of warmth, acceptance, and respect.

GETTING STARTED

When conceptualizing your profile, it may help to consider the following points listed in the text that follows.

Your best effort is required. Begin the process of constructing your profile by considering its purpose and the effect you would like it to achieve. Only a small fraction of available birth mothers will ever glance at your profile. Those that do have often responded to several adoption ads and may view dozens of profiles before selecting a handful on which to focus. Therefore, your objective will be to create the type of profile that will stand out from the others and will allow you to emerge as a serious front-runner. The profile you ultimately create should represent your very best effort. Profiles that are assembled hastily or lack sufficient impact may be quickly eliminated in favor of ones that show more careful attention. Plan on doing several revisions until your profile is as good as you can make it.

. . .

PATTI: *"For some reason, it took us a long time to fully grasp the idea of the profile. We had heard somewhere that it should be just a single page with a couple of photos. So that's what we originally did. Looking back on it, I would have to say that our first version was really pathetic. No wonder we didn't get any responses! Gradually, we came to realize that there is actually a lot riding on the profile. After all, the birth mother has to base her decision on something, and most of the time the profile is the most she has to go on. After this finally dawned on us, we basically started over. We got very serious about it. Our final version was a ten-page booklet with about twelve color pictures. We edited the wording very carefully and fine-tuned the layout until we got it just right. Finally, we were satisfied that it was the best we could offer and gave a bunch to our attorney. He said, 'It looks like you are really ready to adopt.' We connected with a birth mother a couple of months later."*

. . .

Neatness counts. The overall appearance should be attractive and well designed. Avoid handwriting your profile unless your script is exceptional. Many adopting parents find it convenient to create their profiles at home using their personal computer. Once the text and layout is generated, your original photos can then be attached before taking everything down to a local shop for color copying. Another good alternative is to use a scanner to input photos directly into your computer. This way, the entire process can be completed at home. In any case, avoid attaching prints of your photos to your profile. It may be difficult to achieve a clean look with photos that are affixed with glue, staples, or paperclips. Your finished product can be placed in a binder or printed on doublewide paper, stapled and folded in the center. If you take your original to a shop that does color copying, instruct the staff to avoid any extraneous lines or shadows around photo edges. Copies that are mailed to prospective birth mothers should appear "fresh" and in good condition.

Your personal touch is preferred. Some professional services will create your adoption profile for a fee. However, despite any doubts you may have about your own abilities, the reality is that a profile you create is far more likely to be effective than one produced by a professional. Why? Consider the message you are sending to your prospective birth mother. Your profile is viewed as a reflection of who you are. Pregnant women selecting among prospective parents may favor those who take a more "hands on" approach to parenting than those who rely on others for important tasks. Your profile should be uniquely yours. It is difficult to project warmth and authenticity without applying your own personal touch.

Achieve an optimum length. Adoption professionals differ in their opinions on the proper length of a profile. Many suggest a simple one-page letter with one or two photos. Others recommend the assembly of an entire photo album. Usually, the best approach is somewhere in the middle. Single-page profiles are usually too brief and fail to offer enough information or much opportunity for the adopting parents to get noticed. Profiles that are excessively long can be tedious to read. They are also likely to contain redundant wording and mediocre photos that ultimately will dilute your message. The best length for a profile is usually three to four double-sided pages or six to eight pages in total, including eight to twelve photographs. Plan to do several revisions. Clear, concise language often creates the strongest effect. Photos should be carefully culled so that only the best are included. If two photos depict similar images, eliminate the less effective one. Furthermore, the type and photos should be large enough to be viewed easily. In addition, including some "white space" can add to the overall appearance.

Identify your finer points. Try to identify anything that would qualify you for parenthood, contribute to the future of a child, or help distinguish you from others seeking to adopt. Do you work with children professionally or on a volunteer basis? Are there any other adopted children in your immediate or extended family? Do you work at home? Identify the positive features of the area where you live. People who live in northern climates may be able to stress the child-friendly healthy outdoor activities available to them, such as skiing or sledding. City dwellers can highlight the abundance of cultural opportunities or educational facilities. Do you have one single quality that stands out? More than one? It may help to rank them. And remember, the best quality of all is the sincerity of your desire to love and care for a child. Identifying your strengths ahead of time will help you conceptualize your profile. In many cases, the text, photos, and design of your profile can all be fashioned around the positive qualities you have identified. In this way, you will not only be clearly highlighting your strengths, but will in the process send a message that is uniquely yours.

Select your format. Autobiographical profiles vary broadly in overall look and layout. Some hopeful parents offer a general description of themselves on page one and follow up with different pages for different topics, such as home, children, extended family, or work. Some prefer to present their message in the form of "his and hers" letters—one page from Mom and another from Dad. Those with children may choose to present their letters from their kids' perspective.

Several possibilities also exist for displaying photos. In one technique, photos are selected to illustrate various passages of the text. Both appear together on the same page and the text is simply "wrapped around" the corresponding matching photos. Other profiles display multiple photos on a separate "photo gallery" page. An effective approach is to use often a combination of both techniques. For example, the opening page may simply show your first names in large type, a large photo of yourselves (with your children, if you have them), and lots of white space. On subsequent pages, carefully selected photos can be used to illustrate key points in the text. In this case, the text is wrapped around the relevant photos. The remaining photos are then placed on a separate page, often against an attractive patterned background. In addition, there are various ways to make a profile stand out, including the use of different colored paper, fonts, drawings, or "clip art."

Before constructing your profile, it can be particularly helpful to view on-line Web sites of other prospective adoptive parents (see the appendix). Avoid the temptation of using one of these as an exact template for your own profile. Instead, the purpose is to seek inspiration by noting the possibilities in both format and style.

THE POWER OF PHOTOS

The photos you choose to show a birth mother can exert a powerful influence on her first impression of you. Start by examining the photos you already have in your scrapbook—many of these may be suitable for your profile. Or you might like to take some more pictures. It will often take longer to take and to process your photos than it will take to write your text. So it's best to get started on your photos right away.

Why are photographs so important? In psychological terms, visual images offer immediate cues. When we meet somebody for the first time, we tend to search for cues to help us discover that person's personality. While these impressions often prove incorrect later, the truth may never be known if the relationship fails to get to second base. Prospective birth mothers are no different from other people when it comes to processing visual images. Just as others might, the women who view autobiographical profiles often scan photos for visual cues before reading the written words. If a birth mother does not get a good first impression, she may never read the message you have worked so hard to create. Take the time to examine your photos critically before making your final selections. The following guidelines may help you choose the most effective ones:

Use current photos. Birth mothers want to see how you look now, not ten years ago. It is misleading to include old photos, and this violates the first rule of proper communication with your birth mother—honesty. You will most likely meet your birth mother eventually. Avoid any nasty surprises later on by being up front with your photos now. If you have other children, take care to select only the most recent photos of them, which is especially true the younger they are. A birth mother who sees a photo of a baby may conclude that you will not have the energy to care for another one. (If you select photos that include children who are not your own, state this in a caption.)

Resist the temptation of using your old wedding photos. If you were married more than three years ago, your wedding photos are too outdated to include in the profile. If your wedding took place more recently, you may not wish to highlight this fact to your prospective birth mother, as she may prefer couples with more established marriages. Regardless of how attractive you appeared back then, skip the old photos. The photos you include should all be less than three years old. If you must include an older photo, indicate the date taken.

Favor photos that tell a story. The photos that have the most impact are often those that provide more information than simply what you look like. Select photos that illustrate your strengths and the way you live. For example, if you have other children, a photo of you together with your child engaged in a favorite activity is more informative than a simple picture of you or your child alone. Other examples include pictures of you and your pets playing in the front yard of your home, or you and your spouse making dinner in the kitchen. If you lead an active outdoor lifestyle, you might wish to include a photo of you on skis, bikes, or on a hiking trail. If you've identified your oversize backyard as a major strength, you could include a photo of your family having fun in the backyard.

Smile! Eliminate any photos where the subjects are not smiling. This is especially true if you have other children. While all birth mothers know that every kid has his or her bad moments, your profile is not the place to show how unhappy your child can be. Photos of your children should show them smiling, laughing, and having fun.

Be casual. Many birth mothers may have a hard time relating to strangers who are posed stiffly in expensive-looking attire. Formal poses may also suggest a home with little room for fun and spontaneity. The photo of yourself looking your most presentable is often far less effective than the one of your husband holding your son while he gleefully licks cake batter off the spoon. Still, shorts and T-shirts are fine for a lifestyle photo that shows you boating or hiking, but they may be too casual to be featured on page one of your profile. You do not need to have your photos taken professionally. Few formal studio portraits can match the warmth and authenticity of a simple snapshot.

Include close-ups. Try to include several shots where your faces take up at least 50 percent of the frame. Many amateur photographers step back instinctively to take a photo. But in fact, you should do just the opposite. By "filling the frame" with your faces, you are more likely to communicate intimacy, warmth, and personality. You will also give viewers the sense of being there. Reject any photos where you appear to be the size of ants, regardless of how breathtaking the background might be.

Choose the right placement. Give some thought to the order in which your photos appear in your profile. The best introductory photos are those that show you in a casually posed, close-up portrait, wearing dressy casual attire and warm smiles. Save the picture of you and your son festooned with cake batter for another page.

Consider foreground and background. Pay attention to objects in front of and behind you in the picture. Look critically at every detail you see in the viewfinder—be sure they look attractive and are consistent with the message you are trying to convey. Many people are tempted to use photographs of themselves at past family gatherings. However, pictures with foregrounds depicting half-eaten dinners, beer bottles, and dirty ashtrays are likely to convey the wrong message. Also, check to make sure there are no distracting objects in the background, such as tree branches that appear to be growing out of your head.

Quality. Select photos where your faces are adequately and evenly lit. Outdoor lighting often produces the best shots, but can cause squinting or unattractive shadows. One solution is to avoid shooting at midday. With indoor photography, the artificial light used should be just enough to make the scene vibrant while minimizing distracting shadows. Good indoor portraits can also be achieved by using natural lighting from a nearby window. Avoid using any photos where subjects suffer from "red eye." When using a flash, check to see if your camera has a red-eye reduction feature. If not, covering the flash unit with a tissue can help.

More photos, please. As a final suggestion, consider keeping a supply of additional photos on hand. For example, these could be some good pictures that just missed making the final cut. Birth mothers love photos and many of them will ask you to send more. If your profile has achieved its purpose, a birth mother will be inspired to take a second look. Be ready to respond promptly if she asks, and keep those photos coming.

COMPOSING YOUR TEXT

Once your best attributes, photos, and format have all been selected, it's time to create your message. While there are no rules for the type of information you must include in an autobiographical profile, most contain some description of the adopting couple's background, marriage, work, home, other children, extended family, and interests. It is also appropriate to describe the type of life you could offer a child. Some couples may wish to address additional subjects, such as their attitudes toward adoption, religious beliefs, or parental values. However, most birth mothers are more interested in your ability to provide appropriate moral guidance and family values rather than your particular religious affiliation. Therefore, if you choose to mention religion in your profile, it may be best to do so in general terms. You may have the opportunity to clarify this in the future. If you already have a currently approved home study, state this in your profile.

There will be some information you will choose to omit. For example, it is not necessary or even wise to give details about your finances. If you choose to refer to this at all, it is enough to simply state that you are financially secure. Most birth mothers assume you have sufficient resources to raise a child. Because your phone number will be included in your ad, listing your contact information in your profile is optional (although, obviously, it is required if you later decide to convert your profile into a Web site).

Regardless of the form your profile takes, try to make it as enjoyable to read as it is informative. Communicate your best points in a way that is clear, flowing, moving, engaging, and entertaining. Use a critical eye to edit your writing carefully. Plan to take about two weeks to complete your text. Let your writing "rest" a day or two between each revision. Chances are, you will see new ways to improve it after a short break.

Strive to create a finished product with impact, uniqueness, and authenticity. When your profile is complete, make at least five copies and save the originals. You may wish to make additional copies either for prospective birth mothers or for your own personal use. The following guidelines will help you fashion the most effective text:

Divide your text into parts. Consider giving your profile a superstructure by dividing it into sections. Give each section a heading. Information presented in sections appears more inviting than an endless succession of text. And because you have already organized the information, readers will find it easier to read and understand.

Opening paragraph. Like welcoming a new friend to your home, your opening paragraph should be warm and inviting. You may wish to mention how much you hope to add a child, or another child, to your family through adoption, and why. But avoid any negative wording like, "We know this must be a difficult time for you."

Maintain a child-friendly focus. While crafting your words, try to imagine the qualities a birth mother might be attracted to. Most would want their child to be raised by loving, capable, involved parents who are prepared to offer as many opportunities in life as possible. Emphasize anything that might qualify you as great parents. These could include your interests in healthy outdoor activities, work with children, work or activities that involve animals, your experience as a coach or camp counselor, your proximity to good schools, beaches, mountains, or parks. Mention your belief in an excellent education, but avoid dwelling on your advanced degrees. Likewise, take care not to emphasize how much you love your work. A birth mother may worry that you will have insufficient time to spend with her child. Be sure to mention if you plan to be a stay-at-home parent (or if you work at or near your home). But don't worry if this will not be your situation. Many birth mothers are working moms and can easily relate to such a lifestyle.

Avoid emphasizing your wealth. Profiles that dwell on a family's affluence can be a real turn-off for birth mothers. Many birth mothers may have a hard time relating to such an elite lifestyle. Remember, this is not a competition for who has the most material possessions. What really counts is the love and commitment you can offer a child.

Mention your extended family, if appropriate. Birth mothers are interested in the love and stability that extended family offers. If you have such family members who are eagerly awaiting the arrival of your child, say so. It can also be a good idea to mention family pets, providing they are commonly perceived to be child-friendly. Taking care of pets can speak well for your desire to nurture others.

Describe your vision for a child's future. Most birth mothers would like more for their children than the unconditional love of their parents. They would like them to have a future filled with wonderful opportunities. Consider the advantages you could offer and state them in your profile. The possibilities are endless but may include such things as a top education, siblings, a love for music, a strong spiritual foundation, healthy outdoor activities, and travel.

Avoid promising too much. There are some areas where you might like to avoid being too specific. For example, many people choose to address the issue of openness in their profile. A willingness on your part to participate in some type of open arrangement is a good thing. But, if you wish to make any statements about openness at all, it is usually best to keep it brief and non-specific.

Another area where it is often best to be brief concerns the birth mother's financial support. People who are in favor of providing support for a birth mother's medical and living expenses often wonder if they should state this in their profile. If you are pro-support and would like to state this in your profile, feel free to do so, but again, keep it brief.

Now that you have created an effective profile, it's time to set your advertising campaign in motion. But before you continue, review the following points to ensure your profile is really effective.

CHECKLIST FOR CHAPTER 6

- The information supplied in your profile is honest, positive and respectful toward prospective birth mothers.
- Your profile reflects your finer points.
- All of the photos in your profile are standouts.
- The text is easy to read, accurate, and informative.
- Your finished product is your best possible effort.

7

STEP SIX: ADVERTISE

Once your profile and home study are complete, it is time to place your ads. As with other types of advertising, the key to successful adoption advertising is obtaining the optimum amount of exposure for your advertising dollars. Obviously, the more you get the word out, the greater your chances are to connect with your birth mother. Unless you place some limits on your advertising campaign, however, things can get expensive quickly.

When deciding where to place your ads, it is always a good idea to consider the type of media that most birth mothers currently have access to. For example, recent figures from the U.S. Census Bureau 2001 show that only about 42 percent of all U.S. households could log on to the web in the year 2000. While this represents an increase from 18 percent just three years earlier and those who do not have a computer at home may have access to one at school, work, or their local library, the fact remains that that over half the homes in America today do not have Internet access. Furthermore, families with smaller incomes are less likely to have computers than other socioeconomic groups. Therefore, while on-line advertising can be effective and should be seriously considered by adoption advertisers, it may be best not to rely on this media alone. For now, you may wish to combine online advertising with the more traditional newspaper advertising.

COMMON MISCONCEPTIONS ABOUT ADOPTION ADVERTISING

Potential adopters who hesitate to use advertising to search for their birth mother often do so for several seasons. Although many would like to be actively "doing something" to increase their chances for success, some simply don't know the exact steps to take. Others may feel uncomfortable with the thought of interacting directly with prospective birth mothers. In some cases, hopeful parents believe advertising is too costly or will require too much effort. But with guidance from this book and your own adoption professionals, it can be relatively inexpensive and simple to do. Almost anyone can learn to speak with prospective birth parents if properly prepared in advance. (This topic is discussed in chapter 8.) In fact, for many the key obstacle is often one's own misperceptions about the use of adoption advertising.

Concerns over legality. Advertising by individuals wishing to adopt is legal in most states. What this means is that if you happen to live in a state that does not permit direct adoption advertising, you may not advertise in that state but can advertise in others where permitted. (Currently thirty-four states allow adoption advertising. Seventeen states require that advertising be conducted only by licensed adoption professionals. See the accompanying table. To receive information about the most recent laws on adoption advertising, check with your attorney or contact the state's adoption unit, found in the appendix.) In fact, some adopters actually prefer the idea of advertising in areas further from home simply because they wish to have some distance between them and their future birth parents.

States Permitting Advertising

Alabama	Maryland	Pennsylvania
Alaska	Michigan	South Carolina
Arizona	Minnesota	South Dakota
Arkansas	Mississippi	Tennessee
Colorado	Missouri	Texas
Connecticut	New Hampshire	Utah
District of Columbia	New Jersey	Vermont
Florida	New Mexico	Virginia
Iowa	New York	Washington
Indiana	Oklahoma	West Virginia
Louisiana	Oregon	Wyoming
Maine		

States That Do Not Allow Advertising by Non-Licensed Persons

California	Kansas	North Carolina
Delaware	Kentucky	North Dakota
Georgia	Massachusetts	Ohio
Hawaii	Montana	Rhode Island
Idaho	Nebraska	Wisconsin
Illinois	Nevada	

From: National Adoption Information Clearinghouse, "Legal Issues of Independent Adoption," January 2001.

(For more on adoption advertising laws, see chapter 7.)

Fear of potential abuse. Some people may avoid advertising because of the belief that ads can be a breeding place for deception and exploitation. Internet adoption advertising, in particular, has been portrayed in the media as a hotbed for scams and fraud. Prospective parents, alarmed by certain television reports, may feel poorly equipped to detect potential problems. Although the reality is that most responses to advertisements are sincere, occasionally someone may come along who is not legitimate. Fortunately, it does not always take an expert to detect potential difficulties. Many warning signs can be identified simply by using active listening skills and common sense. But by far, the best way to avoid being taken advantage of is to employ a few simple precautions. Adopters who fall victim to scam artists are invariably the ones who fail to do their homework, ask enough questions, or think critically about the information they receive. As a prospective adopter, you will be expected to make many decisions. But the ability to make informed choices will depend on having adequate knowledge about your options in advance.

Some people believe that adoption advertising exerts too much pressure on pregnant women. Concerns also center on the marketing aspect of having to "sell" yourself to a virtual stranger. However, unlike other forms of advertising, adoption advertising does not attempt to persuade. Advertising, like other forms of communication with a birth parent, should never be used to coerce or mislead. Rather, its purpose is to get the word out that people wish to become parents through adoption and would like to meet the right pregnant woman. In fact, when adoption advertisers observe the proper legal and ethical guidelines discussed throughout this book, advertising works beautifully as a method for bringing people together who otherwise would not hear of each other. Without advertising, few hopeful parents have many opportunities to tell pregnant women about their desire to adopt.

Others hesitate to advertise because they believe that by taking the lead, the adoption process will not be sufficiently monitored by professional people. In fact, all legal adoptions *must* be monitored by one or more licensed professionals. Advertising for a birth mother is not the same as a do-it-yourself adoption. It's important to keep in mind that other experienced professionals will be at hand to offer essential guidance and suggestions. You will not be "going it alone." The Fast Track method requires close coordination between you and your team of qualified professionals. These experts will be available to provide feedback and alert you to potential problems.

Belief that advertising is undignified. Some people feel that advertising to locate a birth mother is tacky and that adoption plans deserve more dignity than to be listed in the classified section of a newspaper. Others believe that as an exchange of sacred parental rights adoption should not be initiated on the Internet or in a classified newspaper ad. In addition, prospective adopters can be uncomfortable with what is sometimes perceived as the competitive "beauty contest" aspect of the matchmaking process. The purpose, however, is not to identify winners or losers but to find the most appropriate fit between both sets of prospective parents, based on their own unique needs and expectations. What some people may not realize is that virtually every adoption attorney, facilitator, and agency uses advertising to attract potential birth mothers. At a minimum, most place their own advertisements in the yellow pages of their local telephone directories. And many adoption professionals go much further than this, using the Internet and other advertising methods to attract potential birth mothers. Some professionals employ large marketing budgets, spending $10,000 or more per month in their advertising efforts. Since most adoption agencies and attorneys use some form of advertising to attract pregnant women, why shouldn't adoptive parents? As the adoption attorney

Randall Hicks points out in his book *Adopting in America,* the key to a successful adoption is the sincerity of the relationship between the birth parents and the adoptive parents, not how they discovered each other.

Ethical concerns. Some may be hesitant to advertise because they feel it is too commercial or smacks of "baby-buying." It is illegal in all states to buy or sell a baby, and Fast Track is not a method for buying children. Almost every state prohibits agencies or individuals from accepting payment for "finding babies." Furthermore, payments to a birth mother, including cash or items of value that are not related to the birth, may be subject to criminal penalties. Every state permits adopting parents to pay some "reasonable" fees, though, that are specifically associated with the cost of the adoption. Most states require a written itemization of expenses, such as medical care and attorney fees, which are then subject to court approval. Nevertheless, some prospective adopters will remain philosophically opposed to offering financial aid to birth mothers. The choice to do or not do so often comes down to a matter of one's personal beliefs.

Privacy concerns. Many people hesitate to consider advertising for fear that revealing too much personal information will lead to unwanted consequences. It is true that listing identifying information can result in more than you bargained for. Organizations that collect personal information could sell your personal information to marketers. Worse yet, identity theft is a realistic concern for advertisers who reveal too much, particularly over the Internet. An identity thief can steal the identity of a person three thousand miles away. All that is necessary is a computer, a modem, and access to the Internet.

Fortunately, it is possible to advertise effectively without revealing all of one's personal details. There are many ways for adoption advertisers to protect themselves. Chapter 7 provides simple and thorough instructions for safe advertising both in print and on-line.

Fear of receiving nuisance calls. Some people avoid advertising because they mistakenly believe that many responses will be insincere or bothersome. They may fear that they will not be able to distinguish between legitimate callers and ones who may not be serious. Or they may worry about speaking with callers who seem to have emotional problems and require hours of "counseling." Some also believe that many callers will become a nuisance, calling repeatedly, or at inconvenient times.

The reality is that the overwhelming majority of callers will be genuinely interested in locating the best home for their child. It is very difficult for most women to place this type of call. It is common for callers to appear nervous and embarrassed. Indeed, you will often be considerably more comfortable speaking with them than they will be talking to you. While it is true that a few callers may seem confused or insufficiently motivated and you may receive some "crank calls," fielding responses can be fairly simple when certain guidelines are observed, which we cover in chapter 8. These suggestions combined with guidance from your adoption professionals will adequately prepare you to field responses successfully.

The belief that adoption should be orderly. Some people fear the unpredictability of fielding calls and wish to avoid dealing with any situations that may seem undefined. However, the reality is that few adoptions are predictable. Even experienced adoption workers are reluctant to predict the course of a given adoption. For one thing, large numbers of variables can and do change frequently. But more importantly, whenever human emotions are involved, as they are with adoption, issues can become complicated. It is precisely because of this complexity that you *must* get directly involved. If viewed from the sidelines, adoption can actually seem more confusing than it really is. For one thing, it's hard to fully understand a given situation by relying on intermittent secondhand reports. Also, it's difficult to monitor developments and respond appropriately. Adopting parents who assume a central position in the proceedings will be better prepared to make decisions that are timely and sound.

The belief that adoption shouldn't work this way. In fact, this is the way that domestic adoption works best. Times have changed in the world of adoption. Years ago, referrals were confidential and adopting parents remained behind the scenes until a social worker placed a child in their arms. But today the high demand for infants and birth mothers' greater involvement in the matchmaking process means that passive adopters are likely to wait for years. Prospective adopters are not wise to do little more than hire an adoption professional and await the results. Adoptions work best when prospective parents are informed and actively involved.

The belief that if an adoption is meant to be, it will just happen. Do you believe in magic? This belief is really a form of magical thinking similar to the prelogical fantasies of many children. "If I wish for something hard enough, then it will come true." The reality is that adoption takes more than wishful thinking. So many details must be arranged that very few adoptions "just happen." In many successful adoptions, the elements that come together do so because the adopting parents have personally set things in motion and closely monitored progress.

Belief that your adoption professional should locate a child for you. Many people think that since they are paying their attorney/facilitator/agency to find them a child, they should not have to search as well. The fact is that while many adoption arrangers can help you locate a birth mother, no one can guarantee a child. Furthermore, adoption workers are busy helping large numbers of other hopeful parents. And most must also coordinate a myriad of details related to adoptions actively in progress. Consequently, if you do not take the lead in the birth mother search, you will have to patiently wait, possibly for a very long time.

SOME WORDS OF CAUTION

Despite the benefits of being proactive in your dream to adopt, it is important to recognize several points:

Adoption advertising is not for everyone. Not everyone feels comfortable placing ads to locate a birth mother. Some are reluctant to enter in to what they see as a competition against other hopeful parents. In other cases, it is not the advertising that is bothersome but rather the idea of having to field calls. Adoptive parents can worry that they will say the wrong thing to a birth mother and lose a potential opportunity as a result. In this case, would-be parents can place ads themselves but should consider enlisting the help of an intermediary to field calls and screen potential candidates.

· · ·

JENNY: *"Our adoption consultant recommended that we advertise in newspapers in order to reach a larger population and increase our chances of finding a birth family. So we placed ads in a daily paper in a big city and also a daily paper in a smaller town. Even though we placed the ads, we asked our adoption consultant to answer the calls. After the disappointment and heartache of eight years of infertility treatments, I just didn't think that I had the emotional energy and strength to deal with talking to potential birth mothers.*

· · ·

Adoption advertising is not always effective. Two of the likeliest causes are adoption ads that are ineffectively written and those that are placed in the "wrong" publications. However, advertisers' expectations can play a role as well. Some advertisers expect little response from their advertisements. As a result, they may place a few ads without giving the process proper consideration to ensure best results. Others have been led to believe that adoption advertising is a magic bullet. When calls fail to pour in in a few short days, they experience acute disappointment and discontinue their efforts prematurely. In some cases, advertisers can view their efforts as unsuccessful if they fail to uncover a birth mother who conforms to their expectations in every way, when in fact they may have heard from several very sincere candidates. Adoption advertising is simply another tool available to those who wish to adopt. And with so few tools available for would-be parents, it is no doubt one worth considering.

THE COST OF ADOPTION ADVERTISING

The total cost of adoption advertising can vary broadly depending on the type of ads you place, as well as how long and extensively you advertise. Most people spend at least $500, while some may spend $3,000 or more. Those who wish to keep their advertising costs to a minimum can limit the amount of time they advertise, or the number of media or publications, or both.

To assist you in identifying your best adoption strategy, general information on advertising rates is present below. Be sure to call the publications to receive the most recent rates and do some comparison shopping before placing your ads. Refer to the information in the appendix for newspaper contact information.

Newspaper Advertising Rates

The cost of newspaper advertising varies broadly depending on the paper's circulation, ad size, and the length of time the ads will run.

The types of newspapers to consider are college newspapers, local daily publications, national weekly publications, national daily newspapers, and newspaper networks. Advertising rates are usually quoted per word, per line, or by column inch. Line and column widths vary among papers, so be sure to ask what you might expect in terms of approximate number of words. In general, newspapers with nationwide distribution will have higher advertising rates than those available locally but will also yield the fastest results. Prospective parents who place ads in nationwide daily or weekly papers often find their birth mother within a few months.

College Newspapers

Advertising rates for college publications are usually very reasonable. Newspapers may be published either daily or weekly. Many also offer on-line versions and will place your ad there free or for an additional fee. Average daily per word rates are $4–$6 for a twenty-word ad. Rates for column inch vary between $8–$20 per inch depending on the width of the column.

Daily Newspaper

Average rates can be between $5 and $18 a line per day. Discounts often apply to consecutive or multiple days. Many dailies also publish on-line editions and can include your ad for an additional charge.

National Weekly Publications

Some papers require readers to purchase a subscription while others are offered free of charge. Nonsubscription weeklies, which consist mostly of advertisements, are often referred to as "shoppers" or "pennysavers." These publications can be preferable to daily papers because they tend to remain on hand longer before being discarded. Ads of twenty words or less average $300 per week. Ads forty words or less will average $550 per week.

National Daily Newspapers

Many adoption advertisers are attracted to the wide circulation and convenience offered by national daily newspapers. Expect to spend about $250 per day or $1,000 for five consecutive days. Nationwide adoption advertising also presents some unique legal challenges. Be sure to observe the warnings described later in this chapter if you are considering advertising in these publications.

Newspaper Networks

Newspaper networks are statewide associations of both daily and weekly newspapers. Networks are often comprised of dozens or even hundreds of associated papers. For $100 to $250 per week you can place an ad of twenty-five words or less in many of the newspapers that belong to that network. Before you place your ad in a newspaper network, however, be sure to ask what percentage of the member papers will run your ad. Many affiliated papers will only run an ad providing space is available. Those on a budget can advertise in the newspaper network association in their home state, if legally permissible. Refer to the appendix for network contact information.

The following guidelines can help you keep the cost of newspaper advertising to a minimum:

- Ask the publication if they have discounts, packages, or special rates for adoption advertising. Some papers will offer discounts for ads that appear repeatedly or consecutively within a specified period of time. Other publications will have special rates for adoption advertising.
- Ask your adoption specialist if he or she would be willing to share the cost of advertising if their contact information is also included in the ads. Some professionals will offer to split expenses if you also list their toll-free telephone number.

- Despite the higher rates, it is often more cost-effective to advertise in one nationwide or regional publication than in several local ones. The cost for one week of advertising in *Thrifty Nickel* may be only slightly more than five days of advertising in a few large daily newspapers. Furthermore, weekly newspapers with nationwide coverage may offer the best value of all, since these publications combine wider distribution with a relatively longer shelf life.

On-line Advertising Expenses

Adopting parents can expect to spend between $200 to $400 to create a personal Web site. Total cost will depend on the number of pages and photos included in the site. You can also have your Web site included in for-profit adoption registry sites for monthly costs of $10–$20 or $50–$100 until you adopt. Some sites also offer additional services such as Web site design, usually $150–$200. Regardless of the type of advertising you select, you will need a toll-free phone number.

Web sites and Web pages should include your toll-free telephone number, your attorney's toll-free telephone number, and your e-mail address. However, you may wish to use a separate e-mail address to use solely for your on-line advertising efforts, especially if your regular e-mail address contains any identifying information. One solution is to use the e-mail address of your Web site designer who can also act as a firewall by filtering out any unwanted responses. Another option is to simply get a special, dedicated e-mail address for the sole use of your adoption advertising. Also, some adoption registries offer e-mail addresses for those who subscribe to their services.

CONTACT INFORMATION

One of the keys to creating an adoption ad is to establish how you will be contacted should someone be interested in responding to your ad. Often the type of contact information you will include will vary according to the type of media you select:

Newspaper advertising.
The telephone number or numbers you list should allow callers to easily make contact with you at no expense to themselves. Plan to include no more than two numbers in your ad. If you include only one number, it should be your number. If you choose to list a second number, it should be your attorney's.

Obtain a toll-free number.
Most long-distance carriers allow you to order a toll-free number without installing a second line. When ordering a toll-free number, try to obtain one with an 800 prefix if possible. Some birth mothers may not recognize other toll-free prefixes such as 877 or 888 and will assume incorrectly they will be charged to make calls to these numbers. The number you list in your ad should be a total of eleven digits starting with 1-800. Some carriers may allow you to have a simple 1-800 number if you specify that this will be a business account. If you must use a prefix other than 800, precede your number with the words "toll-free."

The total cost of toll-free telephone service can range between $100 and $300, depending on the length of time you have the service and the extent to which you use it. Plan to start your phone service just before the ads appear and keep it in effect for several months after your child's homecoming. This way you will avoid cutting your birth mother off immediately after the baby is born. The cost of the telephone calls will be between $40 and $75 per month and will depend on the volume of calls and the frequency and length of time you spend speaking with your birth mother.

List your attorney's number.

Many pregnant women who would like to respond to your ads will prefer to talk with you, rather than your attorney, agency or other adoption professional. This may not always be the case, though. For example, birth mothers who are particularly concerned about legal aspects of the adoption process may wish to speak with an attorney first. Ask your attorney if he will allow you to include his toll free telephone number in your ad.

Be available.

Be sure that callers can reach a real person at all times—preferably you. It takes considerable courage for most birth mothers to make that initial call. Many who are greeted by a machine may simply hang up. If you cannot stay at home to answer calls, consider taking advantage of current technology to increase your availability. Many phone companies offer a call-forwarding service that will forward calls to another number. In addition, the growing popularity of cellular phones can make staying in touch easy. Cell phones can receive calls forwarded from your home toll-free number or they can be connected directly to a toll-free line so that you can be reached nearly anywhere you go. If you intend to include your attorney's toll-free number in your ad, check to be sure he will be available to answer calls during the period of time your ads will run. You should also discuss arrangements for contact after hours.

Listing other contact information.

Adoption professionals have different opinions about the additional types of contact information to provide. For example, some may suggest you provide your e-mail address if you have one. Or, if you already have a Web site, you may wonder if you should include this address as well. The best approach is to list only your toll-free telephone number or your phone number combined with that of your attorney's. It is important to remember that the real goal is to talk with a birth mother. Why? Simply put, you really cannot make a true connection with the right birth mother until you actually speak with her. Regardless of how brilliant your Web site is, you will not have the opportunity to achieve true rapport until there is a spoken exchange.

ALL ABOUT NEWSPAPER ADVERTISING

What to Do Before You Place Your Ads

It is best to do some planning before you write and place your ad. The following steps are provided to help you get the best results from your adoption advertising efforts:

Know the law. Before placing ads, check with your attorney to identify states where adoption advertising is currently permitted. Some states allow advertising by licensed adoption professionals only, while others prohibit it altogether. Changes in state laws also occur regularly.

If your state prohibits attorneys from acting as intermediaries, your attorney may be unfamiliar with specific adoption advertising laws. If so, ask him to contact colleagues in other states to check on current advertising laws. In addition, you can receive current up-to-date information about state laws on adoption advertising by contacting a state's adoption unit (refer to the appendix for listings). Those who are considering regional or nationwide publications should be especially vigilant. Contact the newspaper in advance to check on their current policy and get your attorney's advice. Do not assume that your ad is legal simply because a paper accepts it. It could be distributed in states where adoption advertising is illegal. Some newspapers may be unaware of current laws pertaining to adoption advertising. Others take the approach that it is not their responsibility to comply with adoption laws. In fact, as the one placing the ad, it is your responsibility to comply with the law. When in doubt, the safest course is to avoid nationally distributed papers and focus only on local or statewide publications that you know will be distributed in permitted areas.

Target your geographical region. If your finances are limited, advertising in your own state, if legally permitted, can be an economical solution. Although generally less effective, advertising in local publications is usually far less expensive than nationwide advertising. In addition, adoption ads placed locally will more likely ensure that the baby will be born in your own state. This can be a significant advantage for people on a budget.

If you choose to advertise in your own state, carefully consider which part of your state you will advertise in. If you advertise in a paper that is distributed close to your home, your birth mother will likely live nearby. This may not be a concern to many adoptive parents who know they would like to have frequent post-placement communication with their birth parents. Other adopting parents, however, may prefer to keep some distance with their birth parents, or they may simply be unsure where they stand on this issue at this early stage of the planning process.

Select your publication(s). Those seeking to place adoption ads have many different types of publications to choose from. These include daily papers, weekly pennysavers, college newspapers, papers with national or regional circulation, and publications that target specific nationalities. Pennysavers, sometimes called "shoppers," consist of mostly advertising and are published in urban as well as suburban and rural areas. They are usually distributed weekly. In addition, many ethnic newspapers accept adoption ads and can be a good choice for those who would like to target birth mothers of a particular cultural background. (See the appendix for contact information on newspapers around the country.) Consider the following when selecting the type of paper in which to place your ads:

• *Target audience.* Most people might assume naturally that a good strategy is to select those papers that are geared toward young women. As a result, many adoption advertisers initially consider college newspapers. However, the reality is that today's college students have received extensive sex education training and are knowledgeable and concerned about sexually transmitted diseases. They also have easy access to a variety of birth control techniques. And often, many students who do experience an unplanned pregnancy choose abortion over adoption. Despite this, advertising in campus newspapers can be successful, especially if you target a rural college or one with a religious affiliation. It's best to consider this method as another "iron in the fire" and plan to focus your efforts in more mainstream publications.

. . .

ANDY: *"We advertised in a variety of different newspapers ranging from daily larger market papers (Kansas City) to college papers (eastern Illinois) to weeklies (a variety of local newspaper groups in more rural and suburban areas) and pennysavers. We got phone calls from the dailies* (Wisconsin State Journal), *the pennysavers* (Thrifty Nickel) *and the weekly rural papers. I'd say the most calls have come from the weekly shopper/rural papers. We did not receive any phone calls from college papers."*

. . .

• *Circulation.* A general rule of thumb is to obtain as much coverage as you can within the limits of your budget. Compare the distribution and advertising rates of a sample of papers or newspaper networks.

• *Shelf life.* Daily newspapers tend to be discarded quickly. For this reason, advertising effectively in them usually requires placing the ad every day. Weekly newspapers are likely to remain in the home much longer. In addition to their good staying power, many weekly papers also have the advantage of being widely read and relatively inexpensive.

• *Effectiveness.* Various publications may yield different results at different times. Therefore, plan to conduct a simple test before plunging in. The basic idea is to place similar ads in several different papers during the same short period of time, a week or two. Since you must make yourself available to answer the calls personally, it can be just as convenient to run several ads simultaneously. Once you have evaluated the responses to this initial test period, you are more likely to know on which publications to focus your remaining advertising budget.

. . .

BETH: *"We have two children through adoption and we used adoption advertising successfully in both cases. But we learned that you sometimes have to go through a little trial and error to find out what works best. The first time we tried to adopt, we placed an ad in a daily paper in a large midwestern city. We were very happy with the results. I think we got about three or four good calls over a one-month period. This is how we found our birth mom. So when we were ready to adopt again, we thought we could just place a similar ad in the same paper. But unfortunately, our results were not as good the second time around. We didn't receive any calls at all. So we decided to shift gears. We ended up trying a combination of one week in a newspaper network with several months of on-line advertising. At the time, my husband was tinkering with the Internet and he decided to put our profile on the Web just to see if anything would happen. We got two good calls from each source and ended up going with a birth mom from our newspaper ad. The lesson we learned was 'Don't put all your advertising eggs in one basket.' "*

. . .

• *Determine the paper's requirements.* Some papers may require a letter from your attorney that demonstrates that your interest in adopting a child is genuine. Others do not permit any specific references to financial arrangements or ethnic backgrounds. Some newspapers will not permit you to include your phone number, insisting that you use only a P. O. box. However, since one of your goals is to make it easy as possible for a birth mother to contact you, it is best to opt for papers that allow phone numbers.

• *Check other adoption ads.* Before writing your own ad, take note of other adoption advertisements currently appearing in the publications you are considering. Although the ad you create should be unique, viewing other ads can be a great place to start. Therefore, contact the publication that you have selected and ask them to fax or mail you a copy of the classified page where your ad will appear. Another reason to check the adoption ads in the paper you are considering is to determine the number of other ads yours will be appearing with. The presence of other adoption ads can be a good sign. It may mean that other adopting couples or professionals have recommended this paper as one that gets good results. You may wish to avoid using papers with ten or more adoption ads however, unless you are confident yours will stand out.

• *Timing.* You should avoid advertising during the holidays or when your attorney will be away. Other times to avoid are early and late summer, just after the end and just before the beginning of school. For those placing ads in daily papers, Sunday is generally better than Monday. Seasonal differences may also exist. If you live in a warm climate, it is typically somewhat better to advertise during the winter. The opposite is true for those living in chillier regions.

HOW TO WRITE AN
ADOPTION ADVERTISEMENT

The good news is that the process of writing your autobiographical profile has provided you with a good foundation for writing an effective ad. By the time you have finished your profile, you are well on your way to acquiring the two key elements of the most effective adoption ads, compact wording and a clear expression of your positive, unique qualities. It may help to think of your ad as a concentrated form of your profile. Begin this process of distillation by reviewing the special qualities you can offer a child and the unique characteristics that set you apart from others. Select two or three words to suitably describe your top qualities. For example:

Instead of	*Substitute*
"We long to share our large home and small farm (with horses) in the country."	"Farm, horses, country paradise"
"We want to offer a child a life of opportunities, a wonderful home, and the love of our extended family."	"Promise baby love, wonderful future, cousins"

Instead of	*Substitute*
"We enjoy camping, hiking, fly-fishing, and scuba diving."	"Healthy outdoor fun"
"A successful litigation attorney and high school teacher."	"Loving dad, teacher mom"
"If you are considering adoption"	"Considering adoption?"

Keep in mind that the wording of your ad may vary, depending on the method a paper uses to calculate the advertising rate. For example, some papers charge by the line or per word. Others, like many pennysavers, use a tiered system that assigns rates according to various ranges of words, for example, 1–20 words, 21–40 words, or 41–60 words. This system usually offers the best flexibility, particularly when it is combined with a relatively low rate. In this case, you may wish to indulge in longer words or more adjectives. However, if you decide to advertise in papers with the highest rates, your ability to edit will be put to the ultimate test. In these cases, you may wish to eliminate excessive words, use shorter words, or make use of abbreviations and contractions. For example, it is acceptable to abbreviate *California* as *CA* as most people will understand this. If you must abbreviate, however, avoid abbreviating your key words, unless most readers are sure to understand their meaning.

Essential Information in Ads

In addition to being succinct and stating your positive qualities, good adoption ads include other essential information. These are:

A reference to what you can offer a child. Ads that only focus on the desires of the adopting couple can appear needy and one-sided.

AUTHOR'S NOTE

We were reluctant to use the abbreviation for Hawaii (HI) in our ad. We were afraid that some people would not recognize the abbreviation and we wanted no misunderstanding when it came to our primary strength. The ad that we placed in *Thrifty Nickel*, which had a relatively low, flexible rate system, looked dramatically different from the bare-bones four-line ad we ran in several daily papers:

THRIFTY NICKEL

ADOPTION: HAWAII FAMILY wishes to adopt baby. Promise love, wonderful future, healthy living, rural paradise, adoring grandparents, and education. We are caring and easy to talk with. Confidential. Expenses paid. Call toll-free Susan/Scott 1-800-xxx-xxxx.

DAILY PAPERS

Hawaii family promise baby love, wonderful future, grandparents, educ'n. Exp. pd. Sue/Scott 800 xxx-xxxx.

Avoid stating "Please help fulfill our dream of a family." And consider using the phrase "we promise" instead of "we will give" or "we long to offer."

The word "Adopt." Include the word "Adopt" or "Adoption" in your ad even if the newspaper provides an "Adoption" column heading. Many readers can be easily confused, unless you state your intentions clearly. Starting your ad with the word "Adopt" will also put it at or near the beginning of the adoption ads or "Personals" column of the paper.

The word "baby" or "newborn." Since you are seeking a baby, it is acceptable to state this in your ad. It will also provide another cue for those who may still be confused about the purpose of your ad. It is unnecessary, however, to state "newborn baby."

Your first names and toll-free telephone number. Although this may sound obvious, you must include your first names in your ad. Some adopting parents fear they will be unable to maintain their anonymity if they use their real first names. Even if your names are unusual, the chance that anyone could guess your identity is extremely remote. Do not simply state "Please call us at 1-800-xxx-xxxx." Many attorneys or agencies also place ads. Including your first names provides an important clue that you are an individual, couple or family, and not an agency or attorney.

What You May Include in Ads if You Wish

There are many other things you may wish to include in your adoption ad, depending on your personal situation, your philosophy, or your budget. If you're feeling adventurous, you may wish to experiment with creative wording or graphic elements. If you do, consider conducting a trial run in one newspaper only. Evaluate your response rate and make changes if necessary. Additional elements you might include:

A reference to birth mother support. Many potential advertisers wonder whether or not to include an offer of financial support in their ad. For those who object to the idea of paying a birth mother's living and medical expenses, the solution is easy. Simply leave it out. The decision to include a reference to "expenses paid" is a philosophical question that deserves your thoughtful consideration. Avoid stating this simply because of perceived pressure from the competition. If you have any doubts, it's best to leave it out. If you decide to introduce this topic in your ad, be prepared to evaluate callers carefully.

A reference to religious or family values. Adopters for whom religious practice plays a central role in their life may choose to mention this in their ad. In this way, they may more readily connect with a like-minded birth mother. Most birth mothers are more interested in whether you stress strong morals and family values than your particular religious affiliation. Also, making specific reference to your religious background may screen out some potential prospects. Although the decision is ultimately yours to make, if you mention religion in your ad, you may wish to treat the subject in a nonspecific way.

Nice touches. There are some thoughts you might wish to include, if your budget allows. For example, since it often takes considerable courage for pregnant women to place that call, it can help to include "We are easy to talk with" or "We are compassionate, caring, and easy to talk with." Some potential birth mothers also worry about maintaining their privacy. Including the word "Confidential" shows that you will respect their concerns. Finally, many birth mothers find themselves facing difficult circumstances with little or no support from others. Show your willingness to extend a helping hand by including wording such as, "Let us help you."

Borders, graphics, display ads. If your budget allows, you may use special features to make your ad stand out. Borders, bold capital letters, and additional white space can all effectively enhance classified column ads. In addition, some adoption advertisers purchase large display-type ads. These ads often include larger, bolder type or "clip art." Large display ads sometimes may lack the personal feel of an in-column ad. Or worse, they can be overlooked because of their resemblance to those placed by commercial enterprises.

What Not to Include in Ads

Some of the things you should avoid including in your ad are:

Addresses. Avoid listing your street address, e-mail address, or Web-site address.

Financial status. If you are financially comfortable or the member of a distinguished profession, you may mention these facts only if you can do so discreetly. For example, some advertisers describe themselves as "secure." But avoid emphasizing your wealth and status. Some birth mothers may not be able to relate to such an elite lifestyle. Also, dwelling on your financial resources may send the wrong message or attract those with questionable motives.

References to openness. Some adoption advertisers include a reference to openness in their ads. For example, they may say "We want to stay in touch," "Open adoption OK," or "Ongoing contact." The fact that you are advertising your names and telephone number itself indicates that you are willing to consider some degree of openness. In addition, not all birth mothers desire ongoing post-placement contact. Therefore, unless an open adoption is the only type of arrangement you would consider, any reference to it can be safely omitted.

Reference to baby's health. Avoid mentioning that you seek a "healthy baby." Many birth mothers worry that the family they have preselected will back out if their baby is born in less than perfect health. To minimize this uncertainty, some birth mothers, concerned about finding a permanent home for their baby, will avoid ads that mention a child's health.

References to a baby's heritage. Many people are completely open with the issue of baby's heritage. But for some, preferences may exist. If you have specific preferences for the heritage of the child you seek, it is best to avoid mentioning a child's ethnic or racial background in your ad. Instead, wait until your calls come in. Callers who may not be the right match for you might be a perfect match for another waiting family and should be directed to other members of your professional team for further assistance.

Place Your Ad

Before you place your ad, submit it in writing to the newspaper of your choice. Ask the paper to send you a proof for review. In most cases, this can be accomplished quickly and easily by fax. Check the proof carefully for any errors. In addition, the ad should appear neat and clean, with sufficient white space. Notice the arrangement of the words on each line and make adjustments as necessary to enhance clarity. Check your telephone number or numbers to verify accuracy. Once your ad is placed, ask the paper to fax you a copy of your ad as soon as it appears in print, and review it again. Continue to run your ad for the entire period for which you have prepaid, even if you receive a good prospect immediately. Having additional possibilities never hurts, especially during the initial stages of adoption planning.

ALL ABOUT INTERNET ADVERTISING

Families commonly use on-line advertising as a supplement to their newspaper advertising efforts. Some list their information with one of a dozen or more for-profit on-line adoption "parent registry" sites (see the appendix for listings). Others develop their own personal Web site. As a third option, advertisers can also purchase links connecting their personal Web site to one or more of the parent registries. Regardless of the method you select, your Internet advertisement is essentially an on-line version of your autobiographical profile. Therefore, much of your work is already complete.

Although many people find success on the Internet, it is important to exercise caution. Because of the potential for abuse, never proceed with Internet adoption advertising without first engaging the services of a qualified adoption attorney. And never send money to any contacts without first checking with your attorney.

Internet Parent Registries

Many on-line registries feature prospective parents by using the text and photos similar to the autobiographical profile you have already prepared. For an additional charge, some sites will allow you to include additional photos or interactive features such as slides or video and audio clips. In some cases, potential birth parents are able to search the registry database by categories such as family type, activities, occupation, geographic location, and heritage. Consider the following before selecting an adoption site:

Services and fees. Contact the Web site and find out what services they provide. Rates are usually quoted monthly or for a specific period of time, such as three or six months. In some cases, a one-time setup fee may apply. In addition to basic profile hosting services, some registries also offer a variety of advertising-related features, including advice, links to your personal Web site, the ability to edit your pages, a choice of templates, Web page design, scanning, typing, or additional photos. Keep in mind, however, that some Web sites containing parent profiles are actually maintained by adoption agencies, facilitators, or attorneys. In these cases, you may be asked to pay thousands of dollars in exchange for more comprehensive matchmaking and adoption planning services. If you have already engaged competent adoption professionals, it is unnecessary to pay large fees for services you may already be receiving.

Understand your legal responsibilities. Ask your attorney to review your profile before submitting it to the registry. Do not assume that the registry's requirements are sufficient to comply with current law. As the one placing the ad, it is your responsibility to ensure your ad is legal.

Ask for references. Ask the registry to supply you with names and e-mail addresses of those who have recently experienced success through their service. And then follow up by placing a quick note to each of them. Ask how long their site was in place before they connected with a birth mother, what special options they used, and how satisfied they were with the registry service.

Visibility. One of the keys to effective on-line advertising is to ensure that prospective birth mothers will be easily led to your profile. Try searching some of the Internet's top search engines for the keyword "adoption." Select a registry that is at or near the top of these search engine results. Some registries are also linked to other adoption-related domain names that help to divert traffic to the registry. In addition, interview on-line registries to identify ones that increase their exposure by promoting their services to crisis pregnancy centers and hotlines and in magazines, newspaper articles, and TV or radio spots. Once you have identified a registry with relatively high traffic, your goal is to achieve optimum placement within the registry's database. Interview the registry to determine where and how often your ad will be displayed. Because of the large number of families who use these services, some registries are unable to display all the entries simultaneously. Instead, they use a rotation system. Before subscribing to a registry, determine how many times per month your profile will be displayed.

Search features. Parent registries often employ search features to enable potential birth parents to more easily locate individual parent listings within a registry. For example, users can search the database by categories such as families' location, activities, religion, or heritage. Before subscribing to a registry, understand how its search feature works. Try using the search terms that apply to you and notice the number of families that appear. If your profile will be one of a large number from assorted families, consider using different search terms to narrow the field and make your ad stand out.

Photos. Like your autobiographical profile, your on-line profile should contain several excellent photos. The most effective profiles usually contain at least four. However, some registries do not allow photos. Others permit only one photo. These sites should be avoided, unless you can arrange a link to your own larger Web site. Some sites offer the option of including additional photos for a nominal charge. If you can include four to six photos on a registry with high traffic and visibility, you can eliminate the need for your own Web site.

Dedicated e-mail address. Include a dedicated e-mail address in addition to your and your attorney's toll-free number. Responding by e-mail can be a convenient way for birth mothers to contact you. Some will feel more comfortable contacting you electronically than calling you directly, at least initially.

CREATING YOUR OWN WEB SITE

Another option for adoption advertisers is to create a personal Web site that allows you the flexibility of presenting your unique characteristics without having to conform to standard formats used by on-line parent registries. A number of Web authoring software packages are available that allow you to create a Web page. You simply type the text you want and click buttons to make it bigger, bolder, smaller, or italic. Text can also be easily centered, or aligned to the left or right. You can also import a graphic or photo with a quick button click. Your Web site is essentially an on-line version of your autobiographical profile. So, fortunately, much of the actual content of the site, such as text and photos, have already been created. However, some modifications may be necessary to convert it to an electronic format. For example, you may choose to have a home page with links to several content pages.

The home page provides an introduction to your family. It offers a general description of who you are, where you live, and your special characteristics. Included, too, should be a large photo of yourselves with your children, if you have them. You may wish to provide greater details about your lives and your contact information through the use of links to subsequent content pages. For example, separate pages can be devoted to your home, family activities, activities or hobbies, attitudes on adoption, or extended family. A final page might include your additional photos and contact information. You may also wish to format your photos a little differently. Although, several good quality pictures are recommended, it can be difficult for some Internet users to quickly download large photos. Therefore, a good solution is to provide a photo gallery page showing a number of thumbnail photos. Users can then view larger versions of the image by simply clicking on any of the thumbnails.

Unless you are familiar with Web site coding and search engines and their inclusion policies, it is best to hire a competent Web site designer. For three or four hundred dollars, a professional designer can transform your autobiographical profile into an effective Web site and assist you in obtaining maximum presence on the Internet.

Once your Web site has been created, you need to ensure that prospective birth mothers will find it easily. An important step is to promote your site effectively to search engines, indexes, and directories on the Web, the tools that birth mothers will use to find you.

Good representation on the search engines and indexes is the key to getting the return on all the hard work you've put into creating your site. Therefore, to achieve the best presence, your site must be submitted to the right places. Currently, there are only a handful of major search engines (see the appendix). To be added to the database of these search engines within a reasonable time, you have to pay.

In addition to being included in the major search engines, your site should be specifically coded to target potential birth mothers, as opposed to anyone with a general interest in adoption. This is achieved through the proper selection of "keywords," or the key adoption terms, that users will type in under the search function (for example, "adoption" or "child+adoption").

· · ·

JULIE: *"Before we had our Web site, I had been trying to get the word out by mailing flyers. It was a lot of work and was getting pretty expensive. And then one day I was working on-line and had the idea to check out all the high school Web sites in our area. Almost all of them had the guidance counselor's e-mail addresses. I e-mailed a ton of links to our Web site to high school guidance counselors, school nurses, and teachers. I also went to a lot of church Web sites and e-mailed them links to our Web site. While I was at it, I e-mailed religious youth programs, teen outreach centers, and pregnancy counseling centers. I probably sent at least 250 e-mails or more. I love e-mailing the link to our Web site because it's a lot easier than doing the flyers and will save us a ton of money on postage and color copies."*

· · ·

Once effective adoption ads have been placed, you may hear from pregnant woman almost immediately. Therefore, the next chapter will prepare you for just what you may expect and show you how to field calls successfully. But before you proceed, go through the checklist below.

CHECKLIST FOR CHAPTER 7

- Challenge your personal misconceptions about adoption advertising.
- Determine your advertising budget.
- Obtain a toll-free telephone number.
- Check with your attorney to identify states where adoption advertising is currently permitted.
- Select your newspapers.
- Review the adoption ads placed by other prospective parents.
- Create and place a newspaper ad that stands out.
- Consider Internet advertising as an adjunct to your newspaper advertising.

8

⟨❧⟩

STEP SEVEN: FIELD CALLS
WITH CONFIDENCE

Adopting parents often experience mixed feelings when faced with the prospect of speaking with birth mothers. They fear that the phone will ring and they will have no idea what to say. Even worse, they could say the wrong thing. These feelings are perfectly understandable. This chapter will prepare you to field calls with confidence by showing you exactly what to expect and how best to communicate effectively with prospective birth mothers. Although more art than science, most people can learn to speak with callers by understanding a few simple principles. The first key is to understand a little more about the women you can expect to be speaking with.

ABOUT CALLERS

The personal characteristics of pregnant women who may call you will vary broadly. One study found that birth mothers who place their children independently tend to range between seventeen and thirty years old. While it is difficult to completely understand a potential birth mother's emotions, most are experiencing a very stressful time in their lives. They are often afraid, emotional, and alone. While, as a hopeful adoptive parent, you no doubt feel at least some anxiety at the thought of speaking with potential birth mothers, most birth mothers will almost certainly be considerably more nervous than you.

THE PURPOSE OF THE
INITIAL CONTACT: RAPPORT

Another important step in getting prepared is to know exactly what you are expected to do when responses to your ad start to some in. Unfortunately, many people misunderstand the purpose of the initial contact. They believe that when a potential birth mother makes contact, it is their duty to achieve an immediate match, effectively "sealing the deal." But this is not the case. The true purpose is to make contact, develop some friendly rapport, and encourage the caller to call again. And because you are simply setting the stage for future contact, it is best to postpone many of the sensitive questions for later conversations. While the goals of the initial contact are actually very modest, they are important. Your chief task is to encourage the caller to make contact again, either with you, your attorney, or your agency, because if there is no second call, there can be no future relationship. What is the secret to encouraging subsequent conversations? Rapport.

Although most relationships tend to evolve over a period of time, ultimate success often relies on the degree to which rapport is established during the very first contact. Rapport is the feeling between two people that they can relate to each other. People with rapport often recognize something similar about the other. In some cases there is the sense that they share a mutual bond or seek a common goal. In terms of building rapport, the birth parent-adoptive parent relationship is really no different than other relationships. The purpose of the initial contact is to extend a warm invitation to journey together toward a common goal. Although rapport involves the interplay of many subtle dynamics, those unschooled in the art of relationship building can achieve success by observing a few simple rules:

Use a warm, friendly tone. Studies show that perceived personal warmth is a powerful basic attribute that others find very attractive.

Help the caller feel at ease. Allow the caller to collect her nerves by simply listening to you initially or answering a few casual questions. You might try saying, "Thanks for calling. Your call is really important to me. I'm sure you have a lot of questions, but perhaps you would like me to describe a little about ourselves?" If she opts for you to continue, keep your voice warm and inviting. Despite the butterflies you may be feeling, try to sound relaxed. Just as a smile is likely to be met with another smile, you are more likely to put your caller at ease if you also appear comfortable with the conversation. The first question you ask should be a simple one, like where she saw your ad.

Be respectful. The woman on the other end of the line is not a birth mother until she makes a final decision to place her child for adoption. And she must summon considerable courage to place a call that might lead to an adoption. Any pregnant woman who reaches out to you should be welcomed with acceptance, sensitivity, and respect.

. . .

CAROLYN: *"When fielding calls, it really helps to remember that the birth parent who calls might be a lot like you. In fact, they probably feel very vulnerable and equally powerless."*

. . .

Focus on the caller. The focus of the initial conversation should be on the woman who is expecting. Avoid focusing on yourself or the baby. Also, avoid the temptation of viewing callers as an immediate solution to your personal problems. Do not burden her with your infertility troubles or dwell on your own needs. Remember that the woman is more than a vessel for your baby. Like you, she must resolve some personal issues and is asking for help. Show your concern for her, and not just her baby. Ask her how she's feeling, listen to her fears, and reach out to her.

Be honest. Before a woman will place her baby in your care, she must believe she can trust you. Just like you, those who are considering a home for their babies are concerned that things really are as they appear. And like you, she will be trying to assess the validity of the information she receives. Earn her trust by demonstrating that you can communicate openly and honestly. It is possible to have a successful conversation without agreeing to everything a birth mother wants. It is probably premature to make definite plans during this first call anyway. As the two of you get better acquainted, your expectations and requirements may change.

Summon your confidence. Birth mothers frequently admit that they are turned off by the desperation in the voices of those seeking to adopt. Unfortunately, the reality is that many adopting parents have experienced the torment of watching others achieve success while their own family-building attempts have been met with failure. The result is that they feel anything but confident and optimistic. These feelings are perfectly understandable. But the problem is that negative feelings have a way of seeping into speech or written words, and when they do, they can produce a corrosive effect on a newly forming relationship. Therefore, try to consciously suppress your negative feelings when fielding calls. Instead, reserve these feelings for friends, family, and therapists. Remind yourself of the special advantages you can offer a child. Look for opportunities to weave a few of these points into your initial conversation.

Be an active listener. Unfortunately, people often communicate with others without being fully present in the conversation. We may be busy planning our next remark, instead of truly listening to what is being said. When conversing with a birth mother, strive to be an active listener. Show that you are paying attention by occasionally repeating or paraphrasing what she says, using her key words or phrases. Keep your attention focused on the caller, and avoid dominating the conversation. If you ask a question, wait for her to answer at her own pace. If you think of a question while she is speaking, write yourself a quick note and ask her after she has completed her thought. Avoid the temptation to interrupt, supply answers, or finish sentences.

Focus on shared interests. One of the keys to building rapport is to find some common ground with the other person. Strangers seem more familiar once they have identified shared interests. This does not mean that you must agree with everything the caller says. Instead, look for honest ways to connect.

. . .

MARILYN: *"My daughter's birth mother told me she liked to read. So I told her a story about when I was ten years old and I saved up my money to buy books from the Scholastic book club. I don't know if that impressed her, but we did develop a good relationship that lead to a successful adoption."*

. . .

Build an alliance. Many potential birth mothers are in crisis, with little or no one to turn to. Some secretly hope that you are in a position to help them resolve some of their biggest problems. Reach out to her and let her know that you are willing to accompany her on the adoption journey. Tell her that you are in touch with a team of caring adoption professionals who can help her every step of the way. Also, say that you will personally work with her and will recruit help as needed to make the process as easy as possible.

PREPARING FOR THE INITIAL CONTACT

Building rapport will help you set the stage for a productive relationship with your caller. But to feel even better prepared, the following guidelines may be helpful.

Keep it brief. Most calls will average between ten to twenty minutes. No doubt, you will have many questions for any birth mother who contacts you. But remember, if the first conversation goes well, more are likely to follow.

Remember your positive points. Don't forget the things that you have to offer. When considering your answers, keep in mind that many of the things you perceive as relative weaknesses can be presented in a favorable light. If you do not have other children, for example, don't dwell on your inexperience with kids. Instead, let the birth mother know that you have plenty of time and energy to devote to her child.

Do not try to predict the call's outcome. It is extremely difficult to predict the outcome of any initial contact. This is true even for those who have worked in the adoption field for years. Prospective parents often say that they have had a perfectly wonderful first conversation with a prospect, only never to hear from her again. It is common for pregnant women in crisis to hold their cards closely while they size up things. Give every call your best effort, while assuming the attitude that you will either hear from them again or you won't. Once the call is over, move on and prepare to refocus your energy on the next one.

It's okay to say NO. Despite all your attempts to remain flexible, you may occasionally be contacted by a birth mother who you feel you simply cannot accept. You may learn from her description that there are potentially serious legal risks or health problems. Or you may have concerns about her motivations. In some cases, you may simply lack that emotional connection. If you do not hit it off, there is always the chance that another hopeful family will. Any callers you feel are not a good match for you should be referred to your attorney or agency. In this way, some other family can potentially benefit.

The wife of the couple should answer the phone, if possible. Some prospective birth mothers will prefer to speak with a woman, because many of them have had negative experiences with men. Men can field calls successfully, particularly if they appear sensitive, caring, and are mindful of the rapport-building tips mentioned above.

Make a plan for the next contact. If the initial conversation goes well, set up a plan for the next one before getting off the phone. Determine when and how you will speak again. Will it be a phone call, an e-mail, or a meeting? Who will initiate the contact? Get a telephone number where the caller can be reached before you get off the phone.

Encourage good candidates to phone your adoption professional. Callers who appear to be good candidates should be encouraged to call your attorney or other professional. Alternately, you may ask the pregnant woman if your professional could call her. Let her know that the call would be to get some basic information from her and would also give her an opportunity to ask some additional questions. Keep in mind, too, that not all birth mothers will be ready to take the next step. Some may require more time to think things through. If you sense some hesitation, offer to arrange counseling.

WHAT TO ASK

Although you should avoid interrogating a potential birth mother on the first call, it is all right to ask a few important questions. Keep a list ready by the phone. Some extra paper, pencils, and contact numbers of your adoption professional will come in handy as well.

Questions to ask include:

What's your name, address, and telephone number?

How did you hear about us? This is a nonthreatening question that will help break the ice and give you important feedback about the effectiveness of your various ads.

What state are you calling from?

How are you feeling? Have you seen a doctor? This can be a diplomatic way to assess the caller's medical and emotional support system. Some women have not yet received prenatal care. Others are in need of counseling but don't know where to turn. If you suspect this is the case, offer to assist her by putting her in touch with members of your team.

Would you like to hear a little about us? Be prepared to carry the initial part of the conversation. When describing yourself, include the following points:

- *Your personal highlights.* Highlight the positives and describe some of the things you can offer a child.
- *Adoption attitudes.* It is natural for birth mothers to wonder about your attitudes about them and their decision to pursue adoption. They may wonder if you can really love their child. If you have a biological child, you may have to reassure her that you are able to love and treat an adopted child the same way. If you have been touched in any way by adoption, describing your experience with love and enthusiasm can be very reassuring.
- *Can you describe a little about yourself?* Leaving the question open-ended is a gentle way to allow the caller to reveal whatever she feels most comfortable revealing. If you do not hear the answers to some of your more immediate questions it is all right to inquire further, if you can do so diplomatically. But avoid prying for details about sensitive topics. Most of the time, many of your questions will be answered during the course of the conversation. If not, your adoption professional will obtain the missing information.

Some additional questions to ask her include:

How old are you? If the birth mother does not volunteer her age, ask.

Do you have other children? Women with children are more likely to realize the realities of raising children and may commit to an adoption plan more readily.

What do you like to do for fun? Hearing about her interests and hobbies is a good way to learn more about her. You may also discover that you share some interests in common.

Are you currently working? If not, ask, "What did you do in the past?" If she is currently in school, ask her "What are you studying?" The answers to these questions can give you some idea of her interests, level of functioning, and plans for the future.

When are you due? Adoption specialists often prefer to work with women who are in their second and third trimesters. On an emotional level, a woman who is "further along" is more likely to feel committed to an adoption plan. In addition, she has also experienced obvious physical changes that make the reality of her pregnancy difficult to deny. In a more practical sense, offering assistance to a birth mother who is only in her first trimester can get expensive.

Are you working with an attorney or agency? Some birth mothers have done a considerable amount of homework about adoption. In their attempts to learn more, they may have previously contacted one or more agencies or attorneys before answering your ad. If so, there is the possibility that she is talking seriously with other adopting families (and possibly accepting their financial assistance).

Are you married, separated, or divorced? If divorced, when was the divorce finalized? The importance of asking these questions is largely for legal purposes. As with her other answers, you should pass this information on to your attorney.

Why are you considering adoption and what are you looking for in an adoptive family? Listening carefully to her reasons for considering adoption will often reveal information about her circumstances and hopes for her child. Her answers may provide a good segue to your own motivations and attitudes about adoptions and child rearing. The information she reveals may help you identify some common ground.

Can you tell me about the baby's father? By leaving this question open-ended, you are likely to hear things about the birth father that you may not have even thought to ask. If the caller does not volunteer it, you should ask these important follow-up questions:

• *Does he know you're pregnant?* Although many states do not require the written consent of the birth father, he will usually have to be notified that he is the father of a child for whom an adoption is planned. There are many reasons why a birth mother may be reluctant or unable to disclose her plans to the baby's father. She may be uncertain of the father's identity or current location. The legal and practical aspects of the birth father's role are often complex. Do not try to explore these issues yourself. Instead, inform your attorney about any information you receive about the father and let him or her advise you and acquire more details.

• *How does he feel about the proposed adoption?* If the father knows about the proposed adoption he may be opposed to it, indifferent, supportive, or even too supportive of the plan, pressuring the pregnant woman into making a decision she would not otherwise consider. Women who feel forced into their decision may experience a lifetime of regret and grief.

Do you know where the father is? Sometimes a birth mother will volunteer information that will tell you whether he is in the picture and to what extent. If she does not, you may ask, if you can do so gently. If not, let your adoption professional do the detective work on this issue.

How does your family feel about an adoption plan? Other family members can have a profound influence on a birth mother's decision to place her child for adoption. This is especially important if she is young and living at home. Never underestimate the persuasive powers of a potential grandma-to-be. If the prospective birth mother is relatively young, her parents are more likely to play an influential role in her life.

What plans do you have for after the baby is born? Women who choose adoption are more likely to have some educational or career goals. Many will choose adoption in order to attend college or learn a trade. Having a plan for after the delivery is usually associated with a stronger commitment to an adoption. It shows that the woman has a more concrete motive to place her child and is looking realistically at her life after the placement.

Would you like to receive more information about us? If you speak to a good candidate, offer to send her your profile. This way, she will have additional information at her convenience. By supplying something tangible, you become more "real" than merely a voice on the other end of the line. Some birth mothers may reciprocate with photos of her own after seeing yours. It is important to keep in mind that some birth mothers are reluctant to share photos. Many believe they are not looking their best during this time. Therefore, any photos that you receive should be evaluated with this fact in mind. Nevertheless, it is important to receive photos from a prospective birth mother, even though they may resist sending them. As previously noted, visual images often yield many additional bits of information. If a birth mother says she doesn't have any pictures to offer you, you may wish to send her a disposable camera along with a postage-paid, self-addressed envelope. Or you may ask the birth mother's social worker to take her picture.

Do you have any other questions? Callers may remember additional questions once their butterflies are under control. Or their minds may be blank while they are on the phone, but their questions are recalled only after they hang up. Let callers know that they don't have to ask all their questions during your first call. You can talk again once they have had a chance to look over your profile.

Can I call you back in a few days?

SUBJECTS TO AVOID

Do not provide counseling. Adopting parents often worry that they must spend hours on the phone counseling emotionally distraught women. However, most birth mothers are simply trying to sort out their options by learning a little about you, your attitudes, and your home. They are unlikely to reveal their innermost feelings unless you open that door. Therefore, do not go down that road. Unless you are a professional therapist, you are not qualified to do counseling. Even if you are a therapist, there is little to gain by delving into emotional issues during this first contact. (Proceed with caution in later conversations as well. See chapter 9 for more information.)

Do not discuss law or finance. Although adoption planning often involves legal or financial issues, avoid discussing these issues directly with a birth mother. As with counseling, you are probably not qualified to discuss the law. Therefore, if the caller raises either subject, tell her you can assist with medical bills and living expenses, but she needs to discuss the specifics with your attorney. Finances can be an especially sensitive subject. It can often help to have your attorney "run interference" on your behalf.

Avoid sensitive issues. It is perfectly understandable for you to wonder about certain sensitive topics. For example, you may be anxious to know if the woman is taking drugs, smoking cigarettes, drinking alcohol, or eating a nutritious diet. You also may be curious about the birth parents' height, weight, physical attractiveness, or ethnic makeup. Although it is natural to wonder about these things, it is usually not appropriate to ask about them in the first encounter with your birth mother.

Sensitive questions to avoid:

> Are you calling from jail?
> Have you ever been arrested?
> How sure are you about this adoption plan?
> Will you change your mind?
> Why won't your family take the baby?
> Do you have AIDS?
> Are you promiscuous?
> Are you doing any drugs?
> What color is the baby?
> Are you cute? Is the father?
> How much do you weigh?
> How do I know you're telling me the truth?

Instead of asking about sensitive issues directly, try doing one or more of the following:

• *Listen carefully*. Birth mothers often volunteer much of this information. Through active listening, you are likely to get many of the answers to your questions.

• *Ask diplomatic follow-up questions*. If the birth mother raises the subject herself, it may be appropriate to ask a diplomatic follow-up question. For example, if she says "Since I've learned I was pregnant, I've been trying to take better care of myself." You might ask, "When did you discover you were pregnant and what have you been doing differently since then?"

• *Wait until later.* Remember that if the conversation goes well, you are likely to speak with her again.

• *Defer to your adoption specialist.* Adoption professionals have more experience and are better prepared to elicit information about sensitive subjects. He or she will later obtain detailed information through written questionnaires and telephone interviews.

AFTER THE CALL

Once you have spoken with a good candidate, there are several things that you should do.

• *Make notes.* Immediately after a call with a good prospect, take a moment to write out some notes. Try to recall everything the caller said and write as much of it down as you can. Add your notes to a file.

• *Brief your partner.* Once your notes are complete, tell your partner the highlights of your conversation. He or she may pick up the phone the next time the birth mother calls. This way, you avoid asking the same questions needlessly. Update each other as the situation changes.

• *Notify your professionals.* Give your professional team the "heads up" when you receive a promising call. Let your attorney know if and when the birth mother is expecting him to call. Share any information that you have learned, including name, phone, address, due date, marital status, and birth father information.

• *Mail a copy of your profile to the caller without delay.* Attach a handwritten note. Invite her to contact you when she has had time to read everything over. Or let her know you will call her in a few days if this arrangement was agreed upon. By then, she may have thought of additional questions. Include your toll-free telephone number. Or, by prior arrangement, include the address of your attorney or other adoption professional.

WHAT *YOU* MAY BE ASKED

Birth mothers are likely to have a few questions for you. They will be curious about who you are as well as where you live, what you do for work and for pleasure, as well as your attitudes about adoption and your feelings about birth mothers. Most of all, they will be interested in your ability to love their child. Many will also have questions about the adoption process. If you are uncertain about how to respond to any of her questions, it is perfectly acceptable to say, "Let me think about that," "Let me check on that," or "Let me talk with my husband about that and I will get back to you." In some cases, the answers you provide may weigh heavily on a woman's decision to pursue adoption planning with you or to choose adoption at all. Therefore, consider your answers carefully.

. . .

APRIL: *"I was surprised by the number of women who had questions about the adoption process. Many of them were seriously interested in placing their baby, but knew little about just how to go about it. Several asked more questions about the process than they did about us. I told them that we were in touch with qualified adoption professionals that could help them. They seemed relieved and very interested. Several called our attorney within days."*

. . .

HOW TO IDENTIFY POTENTIAL DIFFICULTIES

One of the most important ways to inoculate yourself against adoption problems is to approach any potential adoption situation with a level head. Unfortunately, the eagerness that some have to become parents can produce clouded judgment and a reduced ability to detect red flags. Being too desperate to adopt can make would-be parents exceedingly vulnerable to problems that could otherwise be avoided. Always approach adoption situations with caution.

Birth Mother Fraud

Prospective adoptive parents often worry about the sincerity of the prospective birth mothers they meet. They fear that they could be taken advantage of by a woman who asks for financial assistance without any intention to proceed with an adoption plan. When in fact, most women who say they are considering adoption really are thinking about it. Those who later change their mind usually undergo a sincere change of heart. Occasionally, inappropriate requests for financial help are made simply because a woman does not understand the legal restrictions involved. For example, she may be sincerely interested in adoption but has a false impression about her rights. When this happens, a woman may revise her requests for assistance once she has been properly informed about what she is legally permitted to receive. Some women, though, are interested in something other than adoption. For these, the attraction is purely financial gain (or possibly something else, such as receiving attention). While it is not always easy to tell one situation from the other, many times a woman will say something that will reveal important clues. By communicating with her frequently, you will increase your opportunities to assess the validity of her statements.

. . .

PAM: *"My husband and I experienced one unsuccessful adoption before we were finally successful with the adoption of our son. In the one that fell through, we only spoke with the birth woman a couple of times. As a result, it was very hard to get a proper feel for where she was really coming from. Just before she entered the hospital, she let our attorney know that she had changed her mind. We were not in any position to judge if she was really sincere or if we had been scammed. To this day, we have no idea. But looking back on it, I definitely get the impression that she was reluctant to speak with us while the plans were being set. The second time we connected with a birth mother, our son's birth mom, we all spoke more frequently. After a while I started to look forward to our chats. They helped reassure me that everything was on track."*

. . .

The following statements from a potential birth mother can be red flags:

"I want to get to know you better before I call your lawyer." Women who contact you without a legitimate interest in adoption will prefer to talk with you rather than your attorney or other adoption specialist. They fear that their true motives will be readily detected by those more experienced in speaking with prospective birth mothers. Be careful if any woman tells you that they have had a bad experience with an agency or attorney and prefers to work with you directly.

"I am healthy, very attractive, and am having twins." Women who are out to defraud sometimes lure unsuspecting couples by describing themselves and their situation in terms that are overly positive. They rattle off only the most enticing attributes with no mention of any potential shortcomings. In contrast, most women who are

seriously considering adoption generally feel somewhat insecure about how acceptable they will be to you. They are more hesitant to describe their physical attributes even if they are attractive. Few will make glowing predictions about the health of their baby. Instead, they worry that the baby will be born with a physical defect, however minor, and will consequently be rejected by the adopting family at the last moment.

"My car broke down and I can't get to the doctor." Women who are seeking to benefit financially often describe emergency situations that can only be remedied with cash. Many times, they will also conveniently volunteer their address (for easy payment). The mere mention of financial problems is not necessarily a sign of potential trouble. Lack of financial resources is often cited by birth mothers as a reason for considering adoption. The difference is that a sincere birth mother may describe a tight situation but generally will not ask you to send money immediately. (However, she may ask your attorney.) Refer any questions about finances to your attorney.

"I'm staying with friends and will have to move out tomorrow." Always ask for the caller's phone number and address. A prospective birth mother who is not legitimate may be evasive about supplying contact information. Instead, she may insist on only calling you. Ask your attorney or agency to verify the contact information she gives you.

"I would like to have the baby in your home state." Women who seek money sometimes offer to come to your state simply to obtain a plane ticket. Once they receive it, they may cash it in and disappear. Although some legitimate birth mothers do seek privacy by leaving their home states, most will not ask for a plane ticket during the initial encounter.

"I don't have any questions for you. You sound great and I would really like to work with you." Most birth mothers will not agree to a match during the initial conversation. Instead they will first require

plenty of information about you, including your ability to parent and the type of home you can provide. Then they will need some time to think things over. Those who ask very little about you before agreeing to proceed are likely to be insincere.

Commitment Challenges

Like other potential problems, commitment challenges can sometimes be detected in the first encounter, but will more likely require several contacts to detect with greater certainty, if at all. The following red flags can indicate a commitment problem:

"My mother wants me to keep the baby." Although family members usually do not have a legal right to object to an adoption, they can influence a birth mother's decision, particularly if she is young and lives at home. When the young woman's plans come to light, family members who do not favor adoption may offer to help the young woman if she agrees to keep her child. At that point, a potential birth mother may realize that she has a new set of options, ones that were not available to her when she had originally decided to place her child.

"I just found out I am pregnant." Women who change their mind about adoption are more likely to do so in their first trimester. At this early stage in their pregnancy, most women are considering their options and trying to come to terms with their feelings. In addition, they must manage potential pressure from the baby's father as well as family and friends who may be opposed to the idea. Although no guarantee, it is considered a good sign if a woman in her third trimester appears committed to an adoption plan.

"The father and I are trying to work things out." Many women consider adoption plans for their babies because they are on their own and feel they are not up to the task of parenting a child single-handedly. However, if the baby's father reenters the picture and

offers to share the responsibilities of being a parent, a woman may suddenly realize that her options have changed.

"The father wants me to place the baby for adoption." For an adoption to be successful, both sets of parents must feel in their hearts that the adoption plan is the best option for everyone. Adoptive parents will not wish to be in the situation of taking a child away from a birth mother who is truly opposed to an adoption.

Potential Legal Complications

In some cases a birth mother is deeply committed to adoption, but the circumstances present potential legal difficulties that could be complex. In most cases, the presence of legal red flags will simply necessitate different legal procedures, and will not be sufficient to prevent a successful adoption.

"I don't know who the father is." Birth mothers who have had sexual relations with more than one man around the time of conception may be unsure about the identity of the baby's father. Although the law has provisions for notification and consent in such cases, this situation can be very complex legally.

"I don't know where the father is." If a birth mother knows who the father is but does not know his whereabouts, an adoption can still proceed. However, in this case, adoptive parents run the risk of a father who suddenly reappears claiming his rights to parent. This can occur both before or after a birth mother gives her legal consent. If it occurs before, the adoption may become disrupted. If after, the adoption could be contested by the father.

"My husband is not the baby's father and I don't want to tell him before our divorce is final." Occasionally, a birth mother will be married to one man, but another one is actually the baby's biological father. In this case, two men are involved—one who is the marital

or "presumed" father and the other who is the "alleged" father. A presumed father can have strong legal rights and his consent is usually required. These rights exist even where married spouses are separated, and often for some period after a divorce. Women who are considering adoption but do not wish to disclose their plans to their husband may have to make some difficult choices.

I'm afraid to tell the baby's father about my plans to adopt. Fathers who are unaware of a proposed adoption plan pose a potential risk for adoptive parents. An adoption is unlikely to proceed if the man can prove that he is the baby's biological father, states his objection to the adoption, and sincerely and responsibly pursues his rights to parent his child.

My family is part Cherokee. According to the The Indian Child Welfare Act, an Indian tribe has the right to object to an adoption of any child who is a member of a tribe or is eligible for membership, even in an adoption that is voluntarily arranged by the biological parents. The purpose of the law is to give tribes the right to protect their tribal heritage. Requirements can vary, but most tribes require at least 25 percent Indian blood in the child for eligibility in the tribe. In many cases, a child will be eligible but the tribe will not object to an adoption. Always be sure to mention any possibility of Indian heritage to your attorney. Most qualified adoption attorneys can advise you about any possible risks involved.

Health Concerns

Adopting parents frequently wonder how well a birth mother is taking care of herself during her pregnancy. They worry that she is receiving adequate medical care, is eating properly, and is avoiding drugs and alcohol. In fact, adoptive parents have a right to be concerned, as a birth mother's lifestyle and habits can influence the future health of the child. Yet it is unnecessary to try to extract this information from birth mothers directly, particularly during the initial contact. It is the responsibility of the attorney or agency to do a thorough investigation of a birth mother's medical history. Still, you can be alert to red flags:

"I haven't seen a doctor." It is not uncommon for a birth mother to respond to adoption ads before they have received medical attention. However, if this is the case, mention this fact to your attorney. The quality of medical care that a woman receives is important.

"I took some drugs before, but not since I learned I was pregnant." Any admission of drug or alcohol use is a potential sign of trouble. Pregnant women who use drugs are typically concerned for the health of their child and may decrease or discontinue drug use immediately after learning about the pregnancy. But some birth mothers may not become aware that they are pregnant until their second trimester. If a birth mother says that she discontinued drug use when she learned she was pregnant, ask her when that was. She may be truthful in stating that she quit using drugs at that time, but if she learned about the pregnancy relatively late, then she may have used drugs up to her second trimester. While some may be honest when they say they have stopped using drugs, in other cases, women will have only cut back somewhat. Drug use can be difficult to detect unless a birth mother admits it or exhibits obvious signs, such as confusion, agitation, inappropriate laughter, or slurred speech. If you suspect drug use, notify your professional team and insist that they conduct a thorough medical history.

Now that you can field calls with confidence, it's time to learn how best to maintain contact with the callers who seem most promising. But before you proceed be sure you have completed the following checklist.

CHECKLIST FOR CHAPTER 8

- Establish basic rapport with one or more callers.
- Obtain some basic information about your callers.
- Mail copies of your profile to prospective birth mothers.
- Notify your professional about important leads.
- Learn how to detect fraud and red flags.

9

STEP EIGHT: CREATE A
SUCCESSFUL ADOPTION PLAN

Once you have made initial contact with a prospective birth mother, your adoption journey is not over. In many ways, it has just begun. Promising candidates must be identified. Then, where mutual interest exists, both sets of prospective parents must work together to create an adoption plan that is satisfactory for both parties. Finally, there are practical and emotional tasks that must be accomplished during the period of time leading up to the baby's arrival.

PHASE ONE: AFTER THE
INITIAL CALL

After a first call, there is little to do but wait. Usually some period of time must pass before you learn which prospective birth mothers are seriously considering adoption and, of those, which are seriously considering you. In reality, a number of possible scenarios can occur. Those who are eager to initiate the next step will phone your adoption specialist immediately. Many will wait to review your profile, process their feelings, and learn more about their options. Of these, a few will call you or your specialist after some days or weeks. Still others will respond to additional adoption ads. Unfortunately, most will not be heard from a second time.

Not surprisingly, the unpredictability and lack of control over this phase of the process can often be more than some hopeful parents can bear. Many will be extremely disappointed when good prospects appear to vanish. However, the best you can do is to simply reach out to her during the initial call. After that, it is up to the caller to decide whether to proceed by seeking additional information from either you or your adoption specialist. A pregnant woman must be given sufficient opportunity to consider her next step, especially if she seems unsure about pursuing an adoption plan. She must never be pressured into any course of action. Despite your anxiety, you must refrain from calling prospects back unless you have received permission to call again.

A prospective birth mother who speaks with your attorney or other specialist will be interviewed over the phone. Following this, she will be sent a questionnaire to complete and return. The purpose of the interview and questionnaire is to elicit basic information about a woman's background and medical history and to identify her needs, reasons for considering adoption, level of commitment, and legal circumstances. She will also be asked to sign a consent form giving your professional permission to obtain medical records and proof of pregnancy. Once the questionnaire and pregnancy verification is received, your attorney will advise you of the potential risks of the situation. It's important to note that some women will contact your attorney or agency but will not return the completed forms as requested. Others will follow up with the forms, but for practical or legal reasons may be viewed as "poor risks."

Never arrange a meeting with a candidate or send her money until your attorney has received her completed forms and has verified the pregnancy. It is impossible to assess accurately the legitimacy of any situation until this basic information has been received. However, once a prospective birth mother passes this initial screening process, your journey enters a new and potentially promising phase.

PHASE TWO: GETTING ACQUAINTED

At this point you've achieved an important goal. Even so, it is still unlikely that either you or the woman will immediately commit to a match. The exception, of course, is when the baby's arrival is only a few short days away. (It is not unknown for women to make their first adoption call from the hospital.) In most cases, some time is needed to become further acquainted and evaluate the appropriateness of a proposed match. Several things must be accomplished during this phase. These include: an exchange of information, the establishment of trust, the further strengthening of an alliance, and a mutual understanding about pre- and post-placement contact.

A Word of Caution

When you speak directly with a prospective birth mother, you will be doing two things in tandem. You will be receiving a description from her, which you will evaluate to determine the caller's suitability. At the same time, you will also be offering the caller a description of yourself. Most adopting parents are aware that some callers will not be seriously interested in adoption, or that others, eager to find a suitable home for their baby, may offer misleading information. However, the fact is that prospective adoptive parents are also capable of misrepresenting themselves, either intentionally or unintentionally. Hopeful parents, desperate for a child, can fail to disclose potential problems, fabricate or overstate positive aspects, or make promises they do not intend to keep. In this respect, honesty is a two-way street. The purpose of communicating with a potential birth mother is to exchange accurate information. As prospective parents, your responsibility is to describe yourself accurately so that a woman will have the appropriate information on which to base her decision. Caution should be exercised to avoid offering half-truths or false impressions in an attempt to "sell yourself." Simply put, your goal is to inform rather than persuade. Therefore, in addition to assessing the validity of the caller's statements, you must carefully monitor the truthfulness of your own statements every step of the way. Vigilance is needed to avoid making unrealistic promises or overstating positive qualities. Although honesty with your birth mother is always essential, the period leading up to the commitment and the placement is especially critical. Most of her decisions and expectations for the future will be based on the statements you offer her during this time. By describing yourself honestly, you will be assisting her at a difficult time and building a foundation for a future relationship based on mutual trust and cooperation.

Exchanging Information

Some birth parents may have concerns about the confidentiality of the information they will reveal. Let them know that you respect their privacy and will keep any information they give you confidential. The only exceptions are that you will be sharing information with your attorney, agency, or other adoption professional (to facilitate adoption planning), you will share information with your child in the future, and you will also provide relevant medical details to your child's future physicians. Although the purpose of your contact with a pregnant woman is to get to know each other better, the exact manner in which the information exchange takes place can vary from one situation to the next. Sometimes you will both quickly agree to meet somewhere in person. Other times you will continue to exchange phone calls and letters for a period of a few weeks.

Meetings

Many times a pregnant woman will live nearby, either in your own state or in an adjacent one. If this is the case, it may be convenient to arrange a meeting face-to-face. Although both sets of parents are likely to feel nervous, meetings can often be much more informative than less direct forms of contact. The opportunity to see and greet a person, establish eye contact, and observe nonverbal expressions is likely to yield a far greater amount of information in a shorter period of time. If you both agree to meet in person, you will need to decide where. Some women will not feel comfortable meeting in your home for the first time. In this case, you may wish to select a more neutral spot, for example, a park or restaurant. (If you do meet in a restaurant, be sure to pick up the tab.) Other times, you may agree to meet at your adoption specialist's office. Remember that despite your own butterflies at the prospect of meeting your potential birth mother, the woman is likely to be even more nervous. Break the ice with a few initial remarks or activities. For example, thank the woman for going out of her way to meet you. Let her know how much you appreciate it. In addition, it often helps to bring along a photo album. You can describe some familiar images while the woman is allowed time to settle her nerves. Once everyone feels more comfortable, plenty of questions are likely to follow. Keep the conversation casual and avoid reading questions from a list. If at the end of the meeting there is continued interest, establish a time to talk again.

Letters, Phone, and Electronic Contact

In some cases, it will be appropriate to postpone a face-to-face meeting until more rapport or interest is established. This is especially true where the two parties live in distant states. In this case, a good option is to continue contact through phone, letters, or e-mail to make sure there is a sincere interest in a match before arranging a meeting. If both parties have Internet access, a good deal of information can be easily shared through e-mails, digital photos, and instant messages. Where electronic communication is combined with frequent postal mail and phone conversations, the information exchanged can be plentiful. In these cases, the initial face-to-face encounter may be postponed until everyone meets at the hospital.

By speaking directly with a prospective birth mother, you are in a key position to hear important information about her and her situation. As rapport continues to strengthen, you will find it easier to ask more personal questions that further your understanding about her and her situation. Most adopting parents will be particularly interested in learning more about a woman's reasons for considering adoption, the attitudes of her family and of the baby's father, and her health practices. Any information she offers can be important. Pay careful attention to her statements and ask follow-up questions whenever it seems appropriate. In many cases, you will have to use your best judgment to decide just how far to go with your inquiries. It often will come down to a careful balancing act between your need to know and her level of comfort in discussing sensitive subjects. Keep your antennae finely tuned to monitor her comfort level. However, remember that she, too, will be curious about areas of your life that she perceives to be very personal. For example, she may wonder about your enthusiasm for her and her child, how your other family members view your efforts to adopt, how they will welcome her child, your health, religious practices, or your child-rearing attitudes. Gently opening the door to sensitive topics can give a prospective birth mother permission to ask some questions of her own. The process of information sharing will be more productive if sensitive subjects can be discussed in an atmosphere of respect and acceptance.

. . .

MARTIN: *"We were initially reluctant to ask our birth mother very personal questions. We were afraid that we would phrase things the wrong way and would turn the woman off. We didn't want to take the chance of losing a good prospect. But then as our relationship developed, we finally raised some delicate topics. We asked her about the attitudes of the baby's father and her immediate family. We asked her what she thought would be the most difficult thing about signing the consent forms, when the time came. We asked her how she was taking care of herself and what she was eating. We even asked her if she was currently taking any drugs and whether she had taken any in the past. And to our surprise, we discovered that she seemed very willing to answer all of our questions. In fact, I think she was a bit relieved. Maybe it gave her the green light to discuss a lot of things that were on her mind as well. As a result we all talked more openly, felt more comfortable with each other, and we were able to make a lot of progress with the arrangements."*

. . .

Health Information

Of all the information you receive, some of the most important will be about the health of the birth mother and her child. Pay careful attention to any information she offers. Ask follow-up questions whenever appropriate and listen carefully to the answers. This may be one of the few opportunities you get to address these topics. But be careful not to pry. Unfortunately, some prospective parents are so consumed with these issues that they subject a birth mother to a steady barrage of questions and advice. Sometimes this can stem from the adoptive parents' frustration over their own inability to control the child's prenatal health environment. Or prospective parents may think that since they are assuming the financial responsibility for a birth mother's medical care, she should follow their advice. But birth mothers may become defensive and resentful when questions and suggestions become oppressive. In addition, would-be parents need to remember that health care decisions remain a birth mother's right until she has signed her written consent to the adoption.

While some adopting parents are too aggressive in extracting health-related information about their future child, others can be too reluctant to address these issues. Some may be so eager for a child that they hesitate to explore health issues or are unwilling to hear the answers. Receiving health-related information often requires a fine balance between paying due attention to the information you are offered, without becoming overly intrusive about obtaining or controlling every detail. Instead of prying the information out of her, listen carefully to what she reveals, and monitor her level of comfort with your follow-up questions. Allow her to take the lead.

Determining a Birth Mother's Commitment

Another area of concern for most adopting parents during this initial phase is the birth mother's level of commitment to the adoption plan. Remember that complex emotions are at play for both sets of prospective parents. Most birth mothers are in a time of crisis and will not be functioning at their best. Their behaviors will not always conform to your expectations. In addition, *your* emotions are likely to be atypical as well. Just as hopeful parents who are eager to adopt can overlook signs of trouble, others, more cautious by nature, can easily jump to the wrong conclusion. Therefore, when looking for possible signs of trouble, try to view things in the proper perspective. The occurrence of just one of the signs listed below may not be sufficient to indicate a problem. Remember, that while most adoptions are successful, few of them proceed without any difficulties at all. It is normal to have a few bumps in the road.

The following situations may *sometimes* predict trouble ahead:

Absence of details. Birth mothers who are committed to the idea of placing their baby for adoption are more likely to talk in greater detail about practical aspects of the proposed adoption plan. For example, a woman may volunteer information about her progress in gathering documents or submitting forms. Or she may ask practical questions about hospital arrangements or travel plans.

Infrequent communication. A woman who is reluctant to speak frequently with you or your specialist or who cannot be easily contacted may not be serious about adoption.

Serial noncompliance. Although they will often receive assistance from qualified adoption workers, women who would like to place their babies for adoption must accomplish several steps on their own. They must be seen by a doctor, undergo medical tests, comply with other health care recommendations, sign medical consent forms, complete questionnaires and interviews, and submit requested documents, such as marriage certificates and divorce decrees. Many prospective birth mothers are surprised to learn of all the hurdles they must overcome in order to achieve a successful placement for their child. Obviously, a good deal of commitment is needed to survive the process. When women fail to accomplish one or more of the steps it can signal a lack of commitment.

Missed appointments. Trouble can exist when a woman breaks several scheduled meetings or conversations. Furthermore, a problem may exist if a woman misses several scheduled health care appointments. In this case, she may be trying to avoid seeing a doctor. Women who are using drugs sometimes cancel medical visits in an attempt to avoid detection.

Building an Alliance

A pregnant woman who considers a home for her child must not only evaluate and trust in the information she receives, but she must also feel capable of working with you. She must sense that you care and will be responsive to her needs. The process of building a working alliance starts with the initial call and continues into the getting-acquainted phase and beyond. It is important to approach this phase with a spirit of cooperation.

Contact

The final area that must be addressed concerns the method and frequency of contact both before and after placement. First, you must determine the woman's expectations for contact after the baby is placed. Does she desire a letter and photos once a year? Twice yearly? Would she like to receive videotapes? Does she hope to visit the child on a regular basis? The time to discuss this topic is now, before an emotional commitment is made. Do not assume that her expectations are the same as yours. Always ask. If she says she would like "occasional" letters and photos be sure to define what is meant by "occasional." For some, occasional may mean letters and photos once a year, while others may expect updates every month. Although the details may change somewhat over time, you must ensure that your preferences are basically in accord with hers. Adoptions that proceed without a solid understanding about future expectations can produce lasting difficulties.

In addition, you must agree on the frequency and type of communication prior to the placement. Like you, most birth mothers will feel uncomfortable in the absence of some guidelines. Therefore, by familiarizing yourself with the following tips, you will be better prepared to set the proper pace.

Frequency of contact. How often you communicate with your birth mother will depend on the amount of time she has remaining until her due date. Obviously, things should proceed much more quickly if the baby's arrival is only a few days away. In this case, it may be appropriate to speak daily. If the baby is several months away, communication can take place at a more relaxed pace. In this case, weekly conversations can be sufficient to evaluate a proposed match. However, it is often best to avoid a fixed schedule. Instead, invite the woman to call whenever she has a question. Let the woman know that she is welcome to contact you whenever she needs to. As your relationship develops, you may find communication occurs following important doctor visits or other small milestones in the adoption process.

Method of contact. Although personal meetings will allow for dialogue and often provide the best information, other methods can be very satisfactory, especially if frequency is high. Today's technology allows convenient communication through such electronic means as e-mail, instant messaging, or digital images. When these high-tech forms of communication are combined with phone calls and regular mail exchanges, a strong relationship between prospective parents can develop rapidly.

Limits. Although it is helpful to explore as many issues as you can with a birth mother, a few limits are appropriate. As previously noted, topics to avoid include law and finances. In addition, it is essential to avoid providing too much emotional support. The woman may come to rely on you in the future, which can be hard on both of you as the relationship unfolds. And the birth mother may experience a double loss when the baby is born—the loss of her baby and the loss of her relationship with you as well. Therefore, if she raises emotional issues, express your concern but attempt to "steer clear" by avoiding too many follow-up questions. Simply avoid extending an invitation to explore these issues. Instead, encourage her to seek counseling or to confide in trusted friends or family.

PHASE THREE: COMMITMENT

At some point, both parties must decide whether or not to commit to each other.

Timing

When to Commit
Many adopting parents wonder just how long they should wait before committing to a birth mother. The answer depends on the amount of information you have received and the length of time remaining until the baby's expected arrival. If the woman is only in her first trimester, it may be unnecessary to make definite plans immediately. The more immediate the due date, the more urgent it will be for everyone to agree on a proposed plan.

When You Are Ready, But She Is Not

Birth and adopting parents may not arrive at a decision at the same time. For example, after a few exchanges, you may feel ready to commit to a prospective woman, but she may still be uncertain. Although couples who find themselves in this position are likely to be anxious, it is essential to allow the woman to decide without any pressure or persuasion from you. Under these circumstances, it would be appropriate to continue advertising and holding discussions with other potential leads.

When She Is Ready, But You Are Not

Many pregnant women are eager to locate a suitable home for their baby. Consequently, they may select you as the baby's adoptive parents after only a few days. You must then decide whether to select her in return or to continue your discussions with her while remaining open to another birth mother. For most prospective adoptive parents this decision will be weighty and emotionally charged. Often this moment comes with little warning, despite the long months or years of anticipation. Once a woman has selected you, avoid waiting too long before making your decision. Be prepared to act quickly. This is an anxious time for a pregnant woman. She will likely be nervously awaiting your response and may turn elsewhere if she senses any hesitation on your part. Very few situations will be ideal. A suitable birth mother may not match your every expectation. In most cases, you will be expected to make your decision on far less information than you would like to have. Therefore, you must be willing to accept some ambiguity and proceed on faith to a certain degree. In addition, you should remember that faith, like so many other things in adoption, is a two-way street. The pregnant woman also will not have all the information she desires before making her decision. She, too, must operate on faith. While many adopting parents are struggling with their own decision, it is easy to forget that most birth mothers trust the permanent care of their child to people they have known for only a short time.

Multiple Birth Mothers

Advertising efforts that are particularly effective can often attract more than one promising birth mother. If this happens to you, you will be in the fortunate position of having additional options. Some adopting parents will choose one woman among all the candidates. In other cases, adopting parents will even wish to select more than one birth mother, resulting in the adoption of one or more babies. Although it is not illegal to work with more than one birth mother at a time, ethical considerations do apply.

Precommitment

It is appropriate to communicate with more than one potential birth mother without disclosing the fact to the others. However, this should be done for a brief period only. It is not fair to postpone disclosing your decision unnecessarily. Be mindful of the women's respective due dates. Women who are ultimately turned down must be given sufficient time to find other suitable homes for their babies.

Postcommitment

All of the women must be notified immediately once you have made your selection. If you wish to commit to more than one birth mother, you must disclose your intentions to the women selected. You must tell them you wish to proceed with the adoption of more than one baby and obtain permission from each to be involved in the plan. Prospective birth mothers have a right to know if their baby will essentially be part of a twin set. A pregnant woman who is not made aware of the adoption of another new baby may incorrectly believe that their baby will receive your undivided attention. She must be given the opportunity to ask questions and consider her feelings about this matter before agreeing to proceed with the plan.

If two strong candidates respond to your ads within days, your choices are:

• Decide which woman you would rather work with, based on the information received.

• If you are interested in both women equally, select the woman with the earlier due date. You can proceed to make adoption arrangements with your chosen birth mother while maintaining communication with the other one. This way, if the first birth mother changes her mind, you may still be able to achieve a successful adoption with the second one.

• Seek permission from both women to proceed concurrently. If successful, you will have two babies.

. . .

HEATHER: *"Of all the responses we got from our ads, two women really stood out. Their due dates were four months off, and just a couple of weeks apart. At first we just communicated with both of them. We thought that one of them would naturally drop out or we would discover something that would present a problem for us. But as we continued to learn more about them, they still both seemed very promising. Finally, after about three weeks, one woman informed our attorney that she had selected us. We were a bit caught off guard. We really didn't know that to do. We weren't quite ready to decide between them. Finally we selected the second woman because we had communicated with her more frequently and felt a closer bond to her. The first woman was helped by our attor-*

ney and ultimately found another home for her baby. But having to choose between them was hard, much harder than I had expected."

. . .

PHASE FOUR: AFTER YOU'VE
MADE A MATCH

Once you have achieved a match, your adoption will not proceed automatically. You must work to keep the process on track. To set the stage for a successful placement, you must accomplish three things: coordinate closely with your birth mother and your professional team, manage your emotions, and make a few practical arrangements, such as travel arrangements and health insurance.

Close Coordination

It is essential to stay in touch with your birth mother during this phase. By speaking frequently with her you will continue to build trust and further identify and assist with her needs.

During this phase, members of your professional team will also be speaking with your birth mother. They will be checking on the progress of the adoption arrangements, monitoring her feelings, watching for potential signs of trouble, and assisting with her needs. Communicate frequently with your adoption expert. By coordinating with both your birth mother and your professional, you increase the likelihood that adoption planning will proceed smoothly.

Managing Your Emotions

Stress
The period of time leading up to the baby's arrival is likely to be an extremely emotional one. Your intense desire for a child will mingle with the fear that something dire may happen at the last moment. Excitement and foreboding will seem to coexist in equal parts. This will combine to produce a level of stress that may be difficult to manage at times. It is not unusual to have trouble concentrating on your normal activities, both at work and at home. These feelings are normal for those about to adopt. Use the following tips to keep your stress to more manageable levels:

Express yourself. This is a good time to lean on others for support. Your spouse, other family members, and sympathetic friends all comprise a valuable support system. Reach out to them. Attend adoption support group meetings. Expressing yourself to others is a great way to relieve stress and recharge your emotional batteries. If you don't feel comfortable expressing your feelings to others, jot down your feelings in a journal.

Exercise. Exercise is not only good for the body but does wonders for the mind as well. Exercise improves blood flow to the brain and triggers the release of chemicals known to enhance emotional well-being. Exercise a minimum of three times a week for thirty minutes each time.

Eat right and curb unhealthy habits. (Excessive caffeine, nicotine, sugar, and alcohol consumption will not help you handle stress better.)

• *Caffeine:* Decreasing your caffeine intake during the weeks prior to the baby's birth is a good way for adopting parents to reduce nervous or jittery sensations and enhance sleep, energy, and relaxation.

• *Nicotine:* Nicotine is a drug that produces different short and long-term physiological effects. While the immediate sensation is one of pleasure and relaxation, nicotine's toxicity contributes to increases in heart rate and stress over the long run.

• *Sugar:* Sugar creates a pleasurable short-term effect by temporarily raising energy. However, it also triggers the secretion of insulin which ultimately reduces the amount of sugar in the bloodstream and causes a decline in energy.

• *Alcohol:* While small amounts of alcohol can help you relax, larger quantities can produce disruptions in sleep and other long-term physiological damage. Limit your consumption of alcoholic beverages. Focus instead on healthier means of relaxation.

Get adequate sleep. Getting sufficient sleep is a positive way to combat stress. Without proper rest most people do not cope well with additional stress. With more sleep, most people feel better and are more prepared to cope with the demands of a difficult situation. Improve your sleep habits by going to bed thirty minutes earlier.

Take a break. During stressful times, it is essential to acknowledge the difficulty of the situation and give yourself permission to do something just for you. Take time out to enjoy healthy forms of relaxation, such as seeing a movie, listening to music, or indulging in a massage or a warm bath. Or engage in other leisure time activities, such as recreation, socializing, entertainment, and hobbies.

Practice your faith/meditate. Many people take comfort in their religious practices during life's more challenging moments. Attend services, or engage in prayer or meditation. Participating in restful activities can induce relaxation by slowing pulse, blood pressure, and breathing.

Obsessive Thinking

Most prospective parents, eager to welcome a new child into the family, have incurred a heavy investment in terms of time, money, and emotions. Understandably they are anxious to know the eventual outcome of their efforts. Many tend to dwell on the prospect a bit too intensely. While it can help to monitor developments closely, it is possible go overboard. Some adopters become excessively preoccupied with adoption arrangements. Hoping to avoid failure, they search for the slightest ways to influence adoption events. They may phone their professional team excessively and question every detail. Needless to say, micromanagement by adoption clients can place an additional burden on busy adoption professionals who must meet the needs of other clients as well.

It's difficult to maintain a healthy outlook on adoption proceedings. It is also hard to know just what to expect if you have never adopted before. For those who are unsure of the proper perspective, it can help to observe a general truth about adoption planning— that is, that adoptions are unpredictable. Information tends to trickle in sporadically. It will rarely be sufficient. Be prepared to deal with these realities.

Try to maintain the proper perspective and, most of all, be flexible. Acknowledge the fact that your ability to influence the outcome of an adoption is limited. After months or years of focused effort, it can be hard to know just when to ease off and allow matters to simply unfold. It's important to distinguish, however, between the problems you can influence and those you cannot.

Cold Feet

You have traveled a very long path in your goal to adopt. Finally, the baby's birth is only days away. At this point, you should feel overwhelmed with excitement, right? Not exactly. In reality, many of the soon-to-adopt will feel something distinctly different from excitement—namely, dread, fear, or panic. This may happen to you. Or, you will be excited while your spouse will experience doubts. Some negative feelings are normal.

Most people wonder if they have what it takes to be a good parent. Fortunately, you are not expected to know everything about parenting immediately. Most new parents experience a steep learning curve. You will probably do just fine.

Like other milestones in life, adopting a child will be accompanied by some nervous feelings. After all, few people get married or experience the birth of their first biological child without some trepidation.

TAKING CARE OF BUSINESS: WHAT YOU NEED TO DO BEFORE THE BABY'S BIRTH

Statement of Intent

Prior to the match, you and your birth mother agreed in general terms to the communication that would occur after the placement. Now that the baby's arrival is approaching, it is important to formalize the agreement by putting the details in writing. A signed statement of intent between you and the birth parents, sometimes known as a contact agreement, acknowledges what both parties have agreed to do, specifying the frequency and method of communication between parents once the adoption has become final. Such written contracts are not legally binding in most states, rather, the agreement is a moral one. The chief purpose of such a contract is to avoid misunderstandings by ensuring that both sets of parents have a clear understanding of what will occur in the future.

Although both sets of parents may believe that they will remember everything accurately for years to come, in reality it is common for participants to remember their agreements differently.

What should you do if you and the birth parents cannot agree on the frequency of future contact? Occasionally one or both sets of parents will change their mind amidst the emotions that occur at the time of the baby's birth. In this case, both sides must renegotiate to achieve a solution that is comfortable for all. For example, the birth mother may initially agree to pictures and a letter once a year, but may later ask for more. In this case, a satisfactory solution may be to send pictures and letters twice a year or even more often for a limited amount of time. In some cases, you may wish to ask your attorney to assist if necessary.

Travel Arrangements

If the baby will be born in a different locale, you must make your travel arrangements. Although any type of travel can present difficulties, traveling to adopt a child can be uniquely challenging. You must attend to a million things while feeling simultaneously excited, exhausted, and stressed.

If you will be flying, your outbound trip will be easier if you wait to buy everything you need when you arrive. In addition, hospitals often provide much of the essentials for your new baby, including premixed formula, gauze pads, baby soap, and a myriad of other products. While the paperwork is being completed, you will have time to purchase a car seat, a few clothes, and some blankets.

Airlines
Now is the time to start making your travel arrangements, especially if you intend to make airline reservations. If you know in advance that the baby will be delivered by Cesarean section, you can make

these plans hassle-free. Most deliveries, however, are unplanned. You may only have a due date to guide you. So as a general rule, avoid arriving weeks in advance. The baby may be late. Long stays will unnecessarily tax your pocketbook and your emotions. If the baby arrives early, you can always try to catch a last-minute flight. Last-minute fares can be very expensive, but some travel agencies have arrangements with airlines for lower fares for those who must travel for the purposes of a domestic adoption. In some cases, they may also offer the flexibility to cancel or reschedule trips without penalties. Check with the airline about requirements they may have about flying with an infant. Some require a doctor's note to fly with a child less than seven days old. If you will be making a connection, consider asking the airline in advance to help you arrange a ride on the motorized airport cart.

Accommodations

Anticipate being busy and exhausted. So choose a hotel that is located near the hospital and offers rooms with fully equipped kitchens. Having the convenience of a kitchen in your room will make it easier to eat nutritious meals while staying within your budget.

Tell the reservations clerk that you will be adopting and you may be pleasantly surprised to be offered a discount. Many hotels also offer extended-stay rates that will help make your trip affordable. Alternatively, consider staying at a bed-and-breakfast. Many new adoptive parents enjoy the personal attention they receive in a setting that feels a little more like home. It is not necessary to arrange for a crib. Newborns are generally too small for a crib and sleep more comfortably in a bassinet for the first several months. Some new parents choose instead to purchase a terry cloth changing table pad that when placed inside a drawer can be used to make a cozy infant bed. Later, when it is time to return home, it can be easily folded into your suitcase.

Health Insurance

Adopting parents often believe that their adopted child will not be eligible for health coverage until the adoption becomes final. Under federal law, most insurance companies are obligated to cover adopted children from the moment they are placed in the home. In some states, health coverage starts from birth. Adopting parents are not responsible for hospital expenses incurred prior to a baby's birth.

But they will be expected to pay doctor and hospital expenses once the baby is born. Notify your insurance provider before the baby's arrival. Tell them you plan to adopt an infant and will assume responsibility for the child immediately following his or her discharge from the hospital. Ask the insurer what documents they require. Some insurance providers will ask you to submit a letter from your attorney or a copy of the hospital discharge documents. Keep in mind that some insurance company workers may not be aware of the federal law that mandates coverage at placement. If you experience any problems with your insurer, ask your attorney to intervene, or contact your state insurance commissioner.

You may then submit the receipts to your insurer for reimbursement. Keep in mind that some insurers will not cover medical expenses until your baby is home with you. Many birth mothers have their own insurance that will cover their hospital expenses. For those who do not, ask your attorney to check to see if she qualifies for Medicaid. If so, her hospital bill will be covered. If not, you will be responsible for the hospital expenses.

Hospital Arrangements

As your relationship with your birth mother grows, your discussions are likely to turn to the practical aspects of what will occur at the hospital. As openness in adoption becomes more accepted, it is becoming common for adoptive parents to be actively involved in the birth of their adopted children. In some cases, a birth mother may even ask if you wish to be present in the delivery room. As the due date approaches, you will be told the hospital where the baby will be born. Hospitals often have different attitudes and policies regarding independent adoption. You or your attorney should contact the hospital's social services department to determine its adoption policy. Here are a few things you should determine in advance:

What is the hospital's policy on independent adoption? Will they allow you to visit the baby and birth mother in the hospital? Will you be limited to established visiting hours? Do they require a letter from your attorney before allowing you onto the hospital floor? Will you be permitted in the delivery room if authorized by the birth mother? Will you be permitted to leave the hospital with the baby if the birth mother has signed the consent forms?

What are the hospital's attitudes about adoption? Most hospitals have social workers on staff. One of them will most likely meet with the birth mother during her stay in the hospital. It is not unheard of for a social worker or other hospital personnel to make inappropriate comments to women who attempt to place their babies for adoption. Unfortunately, when this occurs unnecessary stress may be added to what can already be a difficult situation. Try to preempt needless problems with the following suggestions:

• Speak with the hospital social worker. Inform the social worker about the proposed adoption. Find out if hospital staff will be speaking to the birth mother about her decision to place her child for adoption. What are they allowed to say? Does the hospital have a policy that limits inappropriate comments and unsolicited advice from hospital personnel?

• If you live nearby, tour the hospital together with your birth mother. If possible, introduce yourselves to the social worker and other hospital staff. Hospital workers are likely to view the proposed adoption more favorably if they see that both sets of parents are working cooperatively toward a shared goal.

• If the birth mother agrees, can she be placed on a medical/surgical floor after delivery instead of the maternity floor? Awkward questions from nurses and other patients can often be averted by allowing the birth mother to recover on a different floor.

Naming the Baby

Selecting a name for an adopted child is not always the same as selecting one for a biological child. Although you will be choosing names for a boy or a girl (or both if you don't know the gender), there are often other issues to consider.

The child's ethnic background. Consider a child's nationality when selecting a name, even if that nationality if very different from your own. Selecting a name that is congruent with the child's nationality is an appropriate way to affirm the child's origins. Later it may assist with identity formation.

When a birth mother selects a name. Years ago, a birth mother would select the baby's name and the adoptive parents would later call the child by that name. Recently, naming practices have changed. At the hospital, the birth mother will be asked to complete the original birth certificate. She may either use the first and middle names you have selected, or she may choose her own names. Frequently, you will know in advance what she intends to do. If she decides to name the child, you will have a later opportunity to indicate your choices on a second, permanent birth certificate.

When a birth mother suggests a name. Many birth mothers will ask you what name you have selected for their baby. Many times they will happily concur and will use your choice when referring to the unborn baby. However, in some cases a birth mother may ask you to give the child a name that she has selected. You may agree to this, or consider using it as a middle name.

Now that you have created a successful adoption plan, it's time to prepare for your baby's homecoming. But before you continue, complete the following checklist.

CHECKLIST FOR CHAPTER 9

- Do you know what to expect immediately after the initial call?
- Have you exchanged information, established trust, and built an alliance with your birth mother?
- Have you established a mutual commitment with your birth mother?
- Have you made travel and health insurance arrangements?

10

STEP NINE: PREPARE FOR
YOUR BABY'S HOMECOMING

As the baby's arrival nears, you are likely to experience a mixture of excitement and nervous anticipation. However, joy over the imminent arrival of your long-awaited child will likely be tempered by uncertainty over how events will unfold once you are at the hospital. Although each adoption is unique and it is impossible to predict every possible development, two aspects are certain—there will be many demands on your attention, and emotions will be riding high. Therefore, it can help to know what to expect as much as possible before you arrive at the hospital.

Begin your preparation by asking your attorney or other adoption professional to explain exactly what will take place at the hospital. As adoption situations vary, your professional is in the best position to advise you on the unique circumstances of your particular case. The suggestions offered below should be used simply as an adjunct to the recommendations given by your professional. Some of the things you may wish to know include:

Who will be there to assist you? It is extremely helpful to have an adoption expert available to lend assistance while your birth mother is in the hospital. Documents must be properly executed and problems may occur that require expert handling. The person who assists you may be an attorney, paralegal, social worker, adoption consultant, or other experienced professional.

What documents will you need to bring with you? You may be required to bring insurance information or a letter from your attorney addressed to the hospital indicating your intentions to pursue an adoption plan.

When and where will the consent form be signed? Your attorney will advise you on the exact procedure. This should include when, where, and before whom the document will be executed. For example, the birth parent may sign her consent while still in the hospital. Or, in other cases, the document can be executed in the office of an adoption attorney or other professional once the birth mother is discharged.

What are the arrangements for ongoing contact with your professional? Questions or problems can arise while the birth mother is in the hospital. Determine how you will remain in touch with your attorney or other professional during this critical time. Will you be able to reach your professional as needed? Can you be given a number to call after hours?

How soon can you bring the baby home? If you intend to transport the baby into a different state after the baby's discharge from the hospital, the Interstate Compact on the Placement of Children applies. This agreement ensures certain protections for children that will be transported across state lines for the purpose of an adoption. Some states will grant approval before the baby's birth. In these cases, you may be permitted to bring the child home immediately. Other states require you to wait until after the child is born (or after the consent form is signed).

* * *

While it is a good idea to have some understanding of what you might expect at the hospital, keep in mind that the actual reality may be completely different. Often the very best way to prepare is to simply be as flexible as possible.

YOUR ROLE AT THE HOSPITAL

Once you know who will be assisting you at the hospital, the next step is to understand just what is expected of you. In general, your primary role is to offer support to your birth mother. In some cases, this supportive role is a very active one. A birth mother who has become comfortable with you in the weeks prior to the delivery may express her desire to have you present at the birth.

Many birth parents realize how important it can be to adoptive parents to witness the birth of their future child. Yours may look forward to your support during labor and delivery. You may even be asked to act as a labor coach. If you are asked to be present in the delivery room, consider your own comfort with observing the birth. Keep in mind that some deliveries turn into a Cesarean-section birth. If you think you may become squeamish, it is acceptable to decline.

If you are not asked to be present at the birth, try not to be too disappointed. Birth is an intensely painful and personal event. The decision to include you in the delivery room should be left strictly up to the birth mother. Some hospitals have policies that prohibit nonfamily members from being present at the birth. Also, there is always the chance that a birth mother who had originally asked you to attend the birth will change her mind moments before the delivery. Show respect for her and her right to choose by letting her know in advance that it is all right if she does wish to change her mind.

If you do not act as labor coach, there are other ways to support a birth mother during this critical time. Check with your attorney about legal restrictions on gift giving. If allowed, immediately arrange to have flowers delivered to her hospital room. Ask your birth mother if you can bring her anything to make her more comfortable. But perhaps the best way to support her is to simply be present for her.

Although by now you have probably developed a good relationship, in some cases you and your birth parents will be meeting each other in person for the first time. Many birth mothers look forward to sharing this time with you and are all too aware of how quickly it will end. Most birth mothers are intensely interested in your reactions toward her child. Any temporary doubts about her decision to place her child can be eased by observing your joy and happiness toward your future child.

Although you will no doubt be excited to see and hold the baby, you must be careful not to neglect your birth mother in the process. She deserves your special attention and respect. Adoptive parents who ignore their birth mother once the baby arrives risk sending the wrong message. Birth mothers who feel emotionally abandoned at this difficult time may wonder if the concern you previously showed for them was really genuine. Worse, they may question their decision to place their child with you. Be attentive to your birth mother and be certain that her needs are addressed.

While at the hospital, maintain the best relationship with your birth mother by observing the following points:

Understand her emotions. The actual moment when the baby is placed in the care of its new adoptive parents is an extremely emotional one. It marks a beginning for one set of parents and an ending for another. No matter how active she has been in the planning of an adoption, a birth mother is likely to experience many painful feelings as this time approaches. The onset of grief and loss may be accompanied by profound sadness, tearfulness, and agitation.

These emotions can be quite intense. While it can often be uncomfortable for adoptive parents to witness a birth mother's pain, it is healthy for birth mothers to release these feelings. Those who do so in the hospital have made an early start in the grieving process.

In addition, many birth mothers feel considerable anger and frustration at being unable to parent their child. Some will resent the fact that you are currently in a better position to do so. Many times these feelings will remain unspoken. However, in a few cases a birth mother may express her angry feelings, either verbally or behaviorally. For example, a birth mother may make additional demands at the last moment. Or she may air her feelings with a close family member who may then try to influence her decision to proceed with the adoption. In some cases you may be able to resolve matters personally by relying on your best judgment and effective communication skills. However, if you do become personally involved, take care to avoid making promises you either cannot or will not fulfill. You may wish to ask your adoption professional to intervene. Birth mothers who appear very emotional or unsure can also benefit from adoption counseling at this critical time.

Allow your birth mother some time with the baby. Following the delivery, some birth mothers may not wish to see their babies. However, the majority wish to spend considerable time with their child. Although adoptive parents may be understandably nervous to witness a birth mother hold, change, or offer bottles to the baby, they should not feel threatened by this, nor should they try to intervene. Some birth mothers who originally state that they will not see the baby following delivery, change their minds. If this happens, it does not necessarily mean that they will change their minds about the adoption. In fact, many birth mothers who feel confident about their decision to place their child often choose to nurture their babies while they are in the hospital. Most know that it may be the only opportunity they will have to be with their child on a one-to-one basis. Allowing a birth mother to spend time with her baby shows respect for her and the painful journey she is experiencing. Adopting parents should always allow a birth mother some "space," especially if she appears uncertain about her decision. In addition, until she has given her written consent to the adoption, she is legally entitled to do as she wishes.

Anticipate other visitors. Many other people may be encountered in the hospital room. For example, you may have an opportunity to meet the birth father, friends, and family members. In addition, you are also likely to meet adoption professionals who have assisted her with the plans. Many of these individuals will be present to lend support to the birth mother. But others come with the express purpose of meeting you. It is important to greet all visitors warmly. The birth mother will no doubt learn of their appraisals of you. Being accepted by the birth parents' close friends and family can provide an additional vote of confidence during this potentially difficult time. Prepare by asking your birth mother in advance who will be present at the hospital. If approved by your attorney, you may wish to bring some small souvenirs as gifts to the birth mothers' other children, nieces, or nephews.

. . .

PAULA: *"When our birth mother went into labor we received a call from our child's birth father. The baby was two weeks early. We quickly changed our travel arrangements and got there as fast as we could. By the time we arrived at the hospital, the baby was already born. I was fine with that. But what I was least prepared for was the scene inside our birth mother's hospital room. Although she had not told her parents, she must have told just about everyone else. There was a constant parade of friends coming in and out to visit. At times it looked like a mob scene. It was difficult to keep track of who everyone was. The atmosphere inside the room changed from being sad and tearful (in between social calls) to upbeat, even festive (when the friends were there). I don't know what I had expected, but it was not that. In addition, our birth mother frequently held, fed, and changed the baby. I felt very stressed when I saw our birth mother playing with the baby. I was worried that she was bonding too much and would hesitate when it came time to sign the consent form. It wasn't until much later that I realized she had already emotionally committed to the adoption, but was simply enjoying her brief time together before she had to say good-bye. Had I been better prepared for this, I would have been less consumed with my own fears and considerably more understanding toward her."*

. . .

Manage your emotions. The time you spend in the hospital is likely to be busy and exciting. In addition to visiting with your birth mother, you will meet with doctors, nurses, adoption workers, as well as an array of visitors. Everyone will have important messages, tips, and instructions to convey. No doubt the highlight will be seeing your future child for the first time—a moment few adoptive parents will ever forget. Adoptive parents must also face some uniquely stressful situations as well. You may be afraid of saying or doing something wrong in the presence of your birth mother or her visitors. In addition, you may also witness a birth mother's emotions first hand. All of this can be emotionally exhausting for adoptive parents. But perhaps most stressful of all is the uncertainty that most adoptive parents will feel over the birth parents' intentions to sign their consent to the adoption. For many, the stress can seem overwhelming. The following tips can help you manage your emotions during this time:

• *Maintain perspective.* It's important to realize that this period of uncertainty will only last a relatively short time. Most states permit a birth mother to sign her consent prior to seventy-two hours after the birth. In some cases, a mother will take some additional time to resolve her feelings. Most likely, you will know the outcome within a few days. In the meantime, it is important to acknowledge that the birth mother is likely to be just as stressed as you are. Gaining the proper perspective will enable you to better focus on the needs of others around you, and your birth mother will appreciate your ability to show compassion and understanding for what she must cope with.

• *Take a time out.* Some adoptive parents wish to spend every moment in the hospital. However, for others this can be too overwhelming. If you are feeling stressed by the emotions and uncertainty in the hospital, it is perfectly acceptable to remove yourself from the action for brief periods of time. No doubt your birth mother will also wish for some time alone. When appropriate, put a little distance between you and the intensity of the hospital floor. Walk down to the hospital lobby, go outside, or take a brief drive. Your hotel room can be a relative oasis of calm—that is, until the baby arrives. Retreat there as needed. Taking frequent short breaks is a good way to maintain your perspective and recharge your emotional batteries.

• *Get some exercise.* If possible, combine your time outs with some exercise.

• *Attend to your own needs.* No doubt you must be responsive to many different people during this time. In the process, it can be easy to forget to nurture yourself. Pay special attention to your own needs. Maintain your energy by eating right and allowing sufficient time to rest.

• *Contact your professional.* If you feel upset about a sudden change of plans, or you are unsure about what to do in a particular situation, call your attorney or other professional for advice. Rely on their expertise to guide you.

Saying Good-bye to the Birth Parents

Once the consent form has been signed and executed, it will be time to say good-bye to the birth parents. Although the moment marks the beginning of your rights and responsibilities as new adoptive parents, it can be an extremely difficult time for the birth mother. Most birth mothers watch with sadness as you depart with the baby, uncertain when or if she will ever see her child again. In addition, many face changes in the close relationship they have enjoyed with you. Now your lives will diverge. Understandably, your attention will shift toward your child and your future together as a family. However, the change in your relationship with your birth mother can often represent an additional loss for her.

Take the time to express your concern for her and her well-being. Reaffirm your gratitude and commitment to her and the child. Let her know that you have not forgotten the arrangements you have made previously regarding future contact with her. In addition, most are acutely aware that they will be leaving the hospital with "empty arms." A personal gift and card from you would probably be greatly appreciated. (Determine an appropriate amount to spend by checking with your attorney beforehand.) Most birth mothers would also be grateful for a phone call from you as soon as you have returned home. This simple gesture tells her you and the baby have arrived safely. It also shows her that you care about her and will honor your pledge to stay in touch. Also, most birth mothers will cherish any photographs you can send her from your time together in the hospital.

HOSPITAL AND MEDICAL MATTERS

Hospital Notification

Adopting parents who wish to visit the birth mother and the baby in the hospital will usually require a letter of introduction from their attorney or agency. The purpose is to inform the hospital about the proposed adoption and establish your right to be present. Ask for a copy of the letter and keep it with you when visiting the hospital. Without it, it may be difficult to gain access to your birth mother and the baby outside regular visiting hours. Having your copy of the letter handy can eliminate the need to wait while a hospital employee searches for the original.

Length of Hospital Stay

The length of time a birth mother will stay in the hospital will depend on whether she has given birth vaginally or by Cesarean section. Women who deliver vaginally usually remain in the hospital between one to three days, while women who have C-sections may stay a few days longer. Healthy newborns may be discharged after two or three days. However, babies with medical problems must stay until deemed medically stable.

Pediatrician Examination

A pediatrician will examine the baby in the hospital, identify any medical problems, and offer recommendations for follow-up care. When the child is determined to be stable, the doctor will authorize his release. Most of the time, this exam will be performed by a pediatrician on the hospital's staff. But in a few cases, you will be required to select your own pediatrician and arrange for the doctor to visit the child in the hospital. Your adoption professional may be able to assist with a recommendation. Or you can call an adoption support group in that area to receive a list of referrals.

Prior to the baby's discharge, the pediatrician may ask you about your preferences regarding circumcision. Do your homework on this issue in advance so that you will know how to respond if your input is requested. Keep in mind that until she gives her consent to the adoption, the birth mother must consent to this and any other medical procedure. It is a birth mother's right to be involved in the baby's medical care until she signs the consent form. The issue of circumcision, therefore, is usually a joint decision.

Many pediatricians are unaware of who they should talk to when giving feedback about the baby's health and medical care. Many times they will incorrectly exclude the birth mother from these discussions. Adopting parents should ask their birth mother if she would like the pediatrician to discuss the baby's care with her. In some cases, she may prefer to defer this role to you.

Birth Certificate

Before your birth mother is discharged from the hospital she will be asked to complete the baby's birth certificate. Don't worry if she records a name different from the one you have selected. A new birth certificate will be issued once the adoption is approved by the court. The new certificate will replace the original one and will indicate your choice of names.

Medical Records

Your child's hospital medical records are usually released once the hospital has received either the adoption documents or a release form signed by the birth mother. Unfortunately, it often takes a few weeks to receive the records, even once the hospital has been provided with the necessary documents. After you return home with your baby, your pediatrician may wish to contact your child's hospital physician in order to achieve optimum continuity of care.

Discharge

While the birth mother is in the hospital she may be asked to sign a release granting the hospital permission to let you take the baby home. The release may also indicate your responsibility for the baby's medical care. The exact manner in which the baby is released into your care will vary. Some hospitals will allow the baby to leave as soon as her medical condition permits. Others will hold the baby until the birth mother is ready to leave. Some hospitals will not allow you to take the baby until a birth mother's written consent is obtained.

LEGAL MATTERS

The Interstate Compact on the Placement of Children

If you are adopting a baby from out of state, the Interstate Compact on the Placement of Children (ICPC) will apply. The Interstate Compact is an agreement among states that defines an orderly and safe transfer of children across state lines for the purpose of an adoptive placement. The Compact requires each state to have an Interstate Compact administrator as part of the state's adoption unit. The compact administrator's job is to review interstate adoption applications to ensure that the adoption complies with the regulations of both the state in which the baby is born and the state to which the child will be transferred. Although each state has different requirements, in most cases the chief requirement is to provide the child's birth state with the adoptive couple's approved home study.

Once the administrator is satisfied that the adoption has complied with the relevant regulations, the adoptive parents are given approval to bring the child home. For most adoptive parents the biggest concern is the length of time they must wait until receiving approval to bring the child home. Adoptive parents should plan for the possibility that the wait could be more than a couple of days. It can occasionally take as long as several weeks to review and approve the adoption application. Although it is understandable that most new parents would like to return home as soon as possible, Interstate Compact approval is an important part of the legal process, and adoptive parents must stay put until it is received. To do otherwise could jeopardize the adoption. A qualified adoption attorney will do everything possible to ensure the application is processed properly and without unnecessary delay. Before the baby is born the specific regulations of the relevant states will be identified. Once the baby is born your attorney will be prepared to submit the required documents promptly.

Signing the Consent to the Adoption

One of the most important legal aspects of any adoption is the birth mother's written consent to the adoption, sometimes called "surrender" or "relinquishment." While the specific regulations of each state may vary, the procedures for the birth mother's written consent are designed to ensure that she has been fully informed about the adoption process and is not being forced to give her consent against her will. States also vary regarding who must witness the birth mother's written consent. A qualified adoption attorney should ensure that all relevant documents are executed properly.

The Adoption Finalization

Once the birth mother and/or the birth father have signed their consent, a court hearing is set to finalize the adoption. While the procedure is a formality, it is a very important one. A judge will review the home study, recommendations, and an accounting of the expenses. In addition he or she will ensure that the consents are properly executed. You and your child will be required to attend, accompanied by your attorney. The birth parents are not required to attend and are usually not present, particularly if they reside out of town. The actual hearing is generally very brief. Your attorney will advise you if the judge is expected to ask you any questions.

PRACTICAL MATTERS

The Nursery

As soon-to-be adoptive parents it will be difficult to contain your excitement in the final days leading up to a baby's birth. Preparing the baby's room has been eagerly anticipated. However, most adoptive parents report that it is easier emotionally to complete a nursery after their child has arrived. Shopping for cribs, changing tables, and other expensive furniture requires an emotional commitment as well as a financial one. Although most adoptions are successful, if yours happens to be among the minority who fail, your efforts to assemble a nursery could bring an additional toll. You may not wish to complete a nursery until you actually have your child.

Select a Pediatrician

You will need to select a pediatrician to care for your child once placement is made. Adoptive parents, like all new parents, are responsible for their baby's health and should schedule pediatrician appointments for well-baby visits and appropriate vaccinations. This is an especially important decision for first-time parents. You will wish to have the baby examined just as soon as you arrive home. When considering your selection, it can be helpful to ask the doctor what his or her attitudes are about adoption. Most doctors realize that some medical records will be unavailable or will be received only several weeks after placement. Hospitals usually will not give you the baby's records upon the baby's discharge. Instead, they will be obtained later, either by you or your pediatrician or through your attorney's assistance.

Start a Scrapbook

During the course of your conversations with your birth mother you will likely acquire letters, cards, photos, and other mementos. Save everything and place all items in a scrapbook for safekeeping. Over the years these will become valuable keepsakes for your whole family. Most of all, your child will likely view the collection as a vital link to his or her personal origins. Many adopted children have difficulty understanding the circumstances leading up to their adoption. Without a clear picture of their earliest beginnings, a child may conclude that he was defective, unwanted, or rejected. Or he may feel totally disconnected from his birth, feeling as though he simply appeared in his adoptive family in the absence of any meaningful context. Having tangible items arranged in a scrapbook can be an especially helpful way for young children to learn about their beginnings.

Obtain a few necessary items for your child before she is discharged from the hospital. Purchase some soft clothing in an appropriate size and bring one outfit with you to the hospital. Your new child will need clothes to wear home from the hospital. In addition, you must provide an infant car seat. It should be new or in good condition. It is illegal for children to ride in a vehicle without an appropriate child restraint system, and many hospitals will not permit you to leave without a car seat. The hospital also may offer instruction in the basic care of your new infant. Take advantage of their expert tips on feeding, changing, diapering, and many other practical matters. Above all, take plenty of pictures. Fatigue and stress often interfere with the storage of accurate memories. You and your child will later cherish the images from what may ultimately become one of the highlights of your life.

HOMECOMING

The day the baby comes home marks a significant milestone in the life of any adoptive parent. Most have waited a long time for this special occasion and have easily imagined all the positive feelings associated with the fulfillment of a cherished dream—joy, accomplishment, and fulfillment. In fact, the reality of this day is apt to be a bit more complex than anticipated. As expected, you will feel happy and excited. However, you may also feel stressed, agitated, overwhelmed, and exhausted, both physically and emotionally.

Parents, especially those new to child rearing, often struggle to learn the finer points of basic infant care. Most must endure a process of trial and error on their way to learning the best techniques for holding, dressing, feeding, and diapering a newborn. To complicate the picture even further, many new adoptive parents expect that they will fall in love with their child immediately and are disappointed or worried when this doesn't happen. Many parents, adoptive or not, commonly fail to experience love at first sight, and most will not feel like the baby's parents on homecoming day. Bonding is a long-term process that unfolds over months and years as baby and parents share emotional experiences and develop familiarity with one another.

. . .

CHRIS: *"The actual reality of our baby's homecoming was completely different from what I had expected. I had this romantic vision of bliss and happiness, when in fact, I was really a nervous wreck. I was very stressed out during our experience in the hospital, worrying about saying or doing the wrong thing or that our birth mother would change her mind. In the process, I had not taken care of myself and had gotten physically run down. I ended up catching a bad cold. And then I gave it to the baby. He was only three days old. The signing of the relinquishment papers was done in our birth parents' attorney's office. Instead of being a happy time for me, all I could do was sneeze and cough. That's the main thing I remember from that time. I could barely function. Then I felt worried and guilty about giving our new baby my cold. I couldn't believe that we were actually permitted to fly home in that condition. But as soon as we got home we rushed the baby to the pediatrician's. The whole episode was exhausting."*

. . .

MATT: *"I wasn't really able to bond with our son until I got home and in my own environment. We were able to spend time with him in the hospital and the hotel room, but we were so busy I couldn't really focus on the baby then. There was just too much going on. I felt like I was just reacting to a million different things at once. I couldn't really connect with the baby with so many distractions going on. But once I got home, things were quieter and I was in a more familiar setting. That's when the bonding process really started for me."*

. . .

Once you are home with your new baby, it is essential to allow time to rest and recover from the strain of the hospital experience. In addition, you will also need to spend some time alone with your new baby. To help make this important period go more smoothly, consider the following tips.

Discourage early visitors. The first few days after the baby's homecoming are a special time for you and your new family—one that should be experienced alone. Let potential visitors know that they are welcome to visit a week or two after your baby's arrival. Plan to keep visits short. In advance, let visitors know the day and time that is most convenient for you. In addition, let your telephone answering machine take your calls. You may wish to record an outgoing message announcing the news and telling callers when they can expect a call back from you.

Plan some meals in advance. Although new adoptive mothers will not have to cope with physical recovery from labor and delivery, both parents will experience sleep deprivation and the possible aftermath of an emotionally exhausting time in the hospital. Prepare and freeze meals in advance. Or stock up on frozen food that can be cooked easily. If your budget allows, collect takeout menus from nearby restaurants and indulge in some restaurant meals at home.

Recruit some help. Traditionally, after a woman gives birth, grandparents and other family members arrive to assist with meals and housekeeping. But things are often perceived quite differently when a baby is welcomed into the family through adoption. Unfortunately, family members may incorrectly assume that there is no need for assistance. In other cases, friends and relatives may wish to help, but are unsure of just what is needed. In advance of the baby's arrival, identify the type of help you would most like to receive. Talk to your friends and relatives about ways they could lend a hand. For example, they may be able to help out with meal preparation, laundry, or running errands. Their assistance could be a wonderful present for both you and the baby. In addition, you may wish to set aside money to hire other help as needed. For example, a neighborhood teen might be hired to mow the lawn. Or you may wish to temporarily hire a doula (a woman who assists mother and child after the birth).

Hopefully, this book's conclusion signals the end of your own successful journey to adopt. While an important milestone has been achieved, the process of becoming a family will continue for a lifetime. Adoptive parents have special issues to consider. They must encourage strong attachments, stable families, and positive communication about adoption-related matters. Fortunately, successful adoptive parenting often relies on many of the same proactive techniques you used to adopt. That is, actively seeking out useful information and organizations, joining a post-placement adoptive families support group, challenging misconceptions, as well as embracing your own confidence, persistence, and resilience. Take advantage of the many resources that exist to help adoptive families. And above all, continue to rely on your personal commitment and involvement in the years ahead. By doing so, you will enrich the lives of everyone in your family for years to come.

APPENDIX

ADOPTION RESOURCES

The information presented below represents a selective sample of the many organizations and publications that can be of help to prospective adopters and adoptive families. Some specialize in a particular area of adoption such as consumer protection, research, or legislative reform, while others offer information about a much broader range of issues.

NATIONAL ORGANIZATIONS

Adoption Advocates of America
Phone: 847-433-0249
www.theadoptionguide.com/advocate.htm

This consumer protection organization provides education, support, and advocacy for adopting families. It also publishes an on-line adoption advocacy guide.

Adoption Exchange Association
820 South Monaco Parkway
Suite 263
Denver, CO 80224
Phone: 303-333-0845

An adoption support and information organization with a focus on special needs adoption.

American Academy of Adoption Attorneys
P.O. Box 33053
Washington, D.C. 20033-0053
Phone: 202-832-2222
www.adoptionattorneys.org

A national association of attorneys dedicated to practice in the field of adoption law. It was formed in 1990 to improve adoption laws and disseminate information on ethical adoption practices. Membership is by invitation only, based on specific criteria. Prospective adopters can obtain referrals by writing or calling for a membership directory.

American Adoption Congress
P.O. Box 42730
Washington, D.C. 20015
Phone: 202-483-3399
www.americanadoptioncongress.org

A network of individuals and organizations committed to reform and public awareness about adoption issues.

The American Infertility Association
666 Fifth Ave., Ste. 278
New York, N.Y. 10103
Toll-free: 888-917-3777
www.americaninfertility.org

A national nonprofit group offers support and education for those with infertility. Services include information and referral on adoption issues.

Casey Family Programs
National Center for Resource Family Support (CNC)
1808 Eye Street, 5th floor
Washington, D.C. 20006-5427
Phone: 202-467-4441
Toll-free: 888-295-6727
www.casey.org/cnc

Casey Family Programs National Center for Resource Family Support is the information and referral arm of Casey Family Programs, a direct service foundation that provides an array of services for children and families, including information, technical assistance, written materials, and referrals. The CNC has also published a guide to current federal tax benefits for foster and adoptive parents, available at http://www.casey.org/cnc/support _retention/federal_tax_benefits.htm. This 19-page booklet is offered as a document that can be downloaded and printed.

The Evan B. Donaldson Adoption Institute
120 Wall St., 20th Floor
New York, N.Y. 10005
Phone: 212-269-5080
www.adoptioninstitute.org

A national nonprofit policy and research organization devoted to improving the quality of public awareness, policy, and practice regarding adoption issues.

National Adoption Center
1500 Walnut St., Suite 701
Philadelphia, PA 19102
Toll-free: 800-TO-ADOPT
www.nac.adopt.org

Provides information about a variety of adoption topics, including adoptive parenting, adoption financing, infant and special needs, and single adoption. Publications are available upon request.

National Adoption Foundation
100 Mill Plain Road
Danbury, CT 06811

Phone: 203-791-3811

www.nafadopt.org

Provides adoption information with a focus on adoption financing.

National Adoption Information Clearinghouse

330 C Street, SW

Washington, D.C. 20447

Phone: 703-352-3488

Toll-free: 888-251-0075

www.calib.com/naic

E-mail: Naic@calib.com

Offers valuable information about all aspects of adoption, including practices, research, and legislation.

RESOLVE, Inc.

1310 Broadway

Somerville, MA 02144-1770

Toll-free: 888-623-0744

www.resolve.org

E-mail: info@resolve.org

A national nonprofit infertility association, founded in 1974, provides support, advocacy, and information for those experiencing infertility. Also offers fact sheets, physician referrals and local support groups for prospective adoptive parents.

OTHER PUBLICATIONS

The Adoption Guide

www.theadoptionguide.com

Also publishes the *Adoption News* at www.adoptionnews.org. Both online newsletters offer education, consumer protection, and advocacy for adopting families.

Adoption Medical News

1667 K Street, N.W.

Suite 520

Washington D.C. 20006
Phone: 202-293-7979
www.adoptionmedicalnews.com
Offers ten issues per year on medical topics of interest to pre- and post-adoptive families.

Adoption Quarterly
Haworth Press
10 Alice Street
Binghamton, NY 13904
Phone: 607-722-5857
Toll-free: 800-429-6784
www.haworthpressinc.com
E-mail: getinfo@haworthpress.com
Offers articles, research, and book reviews for adoptive parents and professionals.

Adoption TODAY Magazine
246 South Cleveland
Loveland, CO 80537
Toll-free: 888-924-6736
www.adoptinfo.net
Bimonthly magazine offers articles on domestic and international adoption as well as foster care issues.

Adoptive Families Magazine
42 West 38 Street
Suite 901
New York, NY 10018
Phone: 646-366-0830
Toll-free: 800-372-3300
www.adoptivefamilies.com
E-mail: letters@adoptivefam.com
Bimonthly magazine for pre- and post-adoptive families. Also publishes *Adoption Guide*, a yearly magazine with practical information for prospective parents.

PACT Press
3220 Blume Drive
Suite 289
Richmond, CA 94806
Toll-free: 888-448-8277
www.pactadopt.org
E-mail: info@pactadopt.org

HOW TO FIND A SUPPORT GROUP

According to the National Adoption Information Clearinghouse, over 1,000 adoptive parents groups and other support programs currently exist across the country. Some groups maintain a focus on special topics, similar kinds of children, or post-placement parenting issues. However, others welcome anyone with a general interest in adoption. Most groups are organized on a local or regional level, while a handful of national organizations provide groups or other support programs. Support groups may also be listed in your local newspaper or Yellow Pages of the phone book. The following organizations may also be able to assist you:

The North American Council on Adoptable Children
970 Raymond Avenue, Suite 106
St. Paul, MN 55114
Phone: 651-644-3036
www.nacac.org
E-mail: info@nacac.org

Adoptive Families of America
42 West 38th Street
Suite 901
New York, NY 10018
Phone: 646-366-0830
www.adoptivefamilies.com
E-mail: letters@adoptivefam.com

STATE ADOPTION UNITS

This list provides basic contact information for the adoption units in each of the fifty states and the District of Columbia. State adoption units offer information about adoption attorneys and agencies in your state. They also provide specific information about a state's adoption laws and programs for financial assistance for those considering adoption.

Remember, independent adoption is legal in many states, but not all. In addition, keep in mind that although the information listed below is accurate as of this writing state agencies occasionally change their personnel, telephone number, or other information. You can receive the most current information by checking your local telephone listing or contacting the National Adoption Information Clearinghouse.

ALABAMA
Alabama Department of Human Resources
Family Services Partnership, Office of Adoption
50 North Ripley Street
Montgomery, AL 36130-4000
Phone: 334-242-9500
Fax: 334-242-0939
www.dhr.state.al.us/fsd/adopt.asp

ALASKA
Alaska Department of Health and Social Services
Division of Family and Youth Services
Southeast Regional Office
Vintage Park
3025 Clinton Drive
Juneau, AK 99811
Phone: 907-465-3235
Fax: 907-465-1669
www.hss.state.sk.us/dfys

ARIZONA
Arizona Department of Economic Security
Children, Youth, and Families Division
P.O. Box 6123
Phoenix, AZ 85005
Phone: 602-542-4296, 877-KIDS NEED U
Fax: 602-542-3330
www.de.state.az.us/dcyf/adoption

ARKANSAS
Arkansas Department of Human Services
Division of Children and Family Services
P.O. Box 1437, Slot S565
Little Rock, AR 72203-1437
Phone: 501-682-8462,
(toll-free) 888-736-2820
Fax: 501-682-8094

www.state.ar.us/dhs/adoption/
adoption.html

CALIFORNIA
**California Department of Social
Services**
Child and Family Services Division
744 P Street, M/S 19-31
Sacramento, CA 95814
Phone: 916-445-9125,
(toll-free) 800-543-7487,
800-KIDS-4-US
Fax: 916-445-9125
www.dss.cahwnet.gov/cdssweb.
html

COLORADO
**Colorado Department of Human
Services**
Division of Child Welfare
1575 Sherman Street
Denver, CO 80203-1714
Phone: 303-866-5700
Fax: 303-866-4047
www.cdhs.state.co.us

CONNECTICUT
**Connecticut Department of
Children and Families**
Office of Foster and Adoption
Services
505 Hudson Street
Hartford, CT 06106
Phone: 860-550-6578,
(toll-free) 800-842-2288
Fax: 860-566-6726
www.state.ct.us/dcf

DELAWARE
**Delaware Department of Services
for Children**
1825 Faulkland Road
Wilmington, DE 19805-1195
Phone: 302-633-2500
Fax: 302-633-2652
www.state.de.us/kids/adoption.htm
E-mail: info.dscyf@stepdefo.us

DISTRICT OF COLUMBIA
**District of Columbia Child &
Family Services**
400 6th Street
Washington, D.C. 20024
Phone: 202-727-4733
Fax: 202-727-7709
www.adoptivefamilies.com
E-mail: mccook&cfsa-dc.org

FLORIDA
**Florida Department of Children
and Families**
1317 Winewood Blvd, Bldg. 7
Tallahassee, FL 32399-0700
Phone: 850-488-8000,
(toll-free) 800-96-ADOPT
Fax: 850-488-0751
www5.myflorida.com/cf_web/my
florida2/healthhuman/adoption
E-mail: des-osc@dus.stak.sl.us

GEORGIA
**Georgia Department of Human
Resources**
Division of Children and Family
Services

2 Peachtree Street NW,
 Suite 8-400
Atlanta, GA 30303-3142
Phone: 404-657-3550,
 (toll-free) 800-603-1322
Fax: 404-657-9498
www.adoptions.dhr.state.ga.us/
E-mail: adoption@dhr.state.ga.us

HAWAII

**Hawaii Department of Human
 Services**
1390 Miller Street, Room 209
Honolulu, HI 96813
Phone: 808-586-5698
Fax: 808-586-4806
www.state.hi.us/dhs/index.html

IDAHO

**Idaho Department of Health and
 Welfare**
Division of Family and
 Community Services
P.O. Box 83720
Boise, ID 83720-0036
Phone: 208-334-5697
Fax: 208-334-6664
www2.state.id.us/dhw/Adoption
E-mail: dhwinfo@idhw.state.id.us

ILLINOIS

**Illinois Department of Children
 and Family Services**
Division of Foster Care and
 Permanency Services
406 East Monroe Street,
 Station #225

Springfield, IL 62701-1498
Phone: 217-785-2509
Fax: 217-524-3966
www.state.il.us/dcfs

INDIANA

**Indiana Division of Family and
 Children**
Indian Foster Care Adoption
 Association
402 West Washington Street,
 W-364
Indianapolis, IN 46201
Phone: 1-888-25-ADOPT
Fax: 317-232-4436
www.in.gov/fssa/adoption/index.html
E-mail: adoptive@iquest.net

IOWA

**Iowa Department of Human
 Services**
Division of Adult, Children, and
 Family Services
Hoover State Office Building,
 5th Floor
Des Moines, IA 50319
Phone: 515-281-5521,
 (toll-free) 800-972-2017
Fax: 515-281-4597
www.dhs.state.ia.us/ACFS/
 ACFS.asp

KANSAS

**Kansas Department of Social and
 Rehabilitation Services**
Children and Family Policy
 Division

915 SW Harrison, 5th Floor
Topeka, KS 66612
Phone: 785-296-3959
Fax: 785-296-2173
www.srskansas.org

KENTUCKY
**Kentucky Cabinet for Families
and Children**
275 East Main Street
Frankfort, KY 40621
Phone: 502-564-7130
Fax: 502-564-3866
www.cfc.state.ky.us/help/
adoption.asp

LOUISIANA
**Louisiana Department of Social
Services**
Office of Community Services
P.O. Box 3318
Baton Rouge, LA 70821
Phone: 225-342-9922,
(toll-free) 800-259-2456
Fax: 225-342-9087
www.dss.state.la.us/offocs/
index.htm
E-mail: webmaster@dss.state.la.us

MAINE
**Maine Department of Human
Services**
Bureau of Child and Family
Services
35 Anthony Avenue
Augusta, ME 04330

Phone: 207-624-8000 (toll-free)
800-452-1926
Fax: 207-287-5282
www.adoptuskids.org/state@ms/

MARYLAND
**Maryland Department of Human
Resources**
Social Services Administration
311 W. Saratoga Street
Baltimore, MD 21201
Phone: 410-767-7506,
(toll-free) 800-332-6347
Fax: 410-767-7506
www.dhr.state.md.us/ssa/
adopt.htm
E-mail: dhrhelp@dhr.state.md.us

MASSACHUSETTS
**Massachusetts Department of
Social Services**
1 Ashburton Plaza, Room 1111
Boston, MA 02108
Phone: 617-727-7030,
(toll-free) 800-543-7508
Fax: 617-742-4528
www.state.ma.us/dss/Adoption/
AD_Overview.htm
E-mail: cis@sec.state.ma.us

MICHIGAN
**Michigan Family Independence
Agency**
Child and Family Services
Administration
P.O. Box 30037

Lansing, MI 48909
Phone: 517-373-2035
Fax: 517-335-6101
www.michigan.gov/fia
E-mail: fiaweb@michigan.gov

MINNESOTA
Minnesota Department of Human Services
Children's Services
444 Lafayette Road North
St. Paul, MN 55101
Phone: 651-297-3933
Fax: 651-296-5430
www.dhs.state.mn.us/CFS/default.htm

MISSISSIPPI
Mississippi Department of Human Services
Division of Family and Child Services
750 North State Street
Jackson, MS 39202
Phone: 601-359-4407,
(toll free) 800-821-9157
Fax: 601-359-2525
www.mdhs.state.ms.us/fcs_adopt.html

MISSOURI
Missouri Department of Social Services
Division of Family Services
P.O. Box 1527
Jefferson City, MO 65102-1527

Phone: 573-751-4815
Fax: 573-526-3971
www.dss.state.mo.us/dfs/adopt.htm

MONTANA
Montana Department of Public Health and Human Services
P.O. Box 4210
Helena, MT 59604-4210
Phone: 406-444-5622
Fax: 406-444-1970
www.dphhs.state.mt.us

NEBRASKA
Nebraska Department of Health and Human Services
Division of Protection and Safety
P.O. Box 95044
Lincoln, NE 68509-5044
Phone: 402-471-2306
Fax: 402-471-9034
www.hhs.state.ne.us/adp/adpindex.htm

NEVADA
Nevada Department of Human Resources
Division of Child and Family Services
610 Belrose
Las Vegas, NV 89107
Phone: 702-486-6178
Fax: 702-486-7626
dcfs.state.nv.us/page33.html

NEW HAMPSHIRE
**New Hampshire Department
of Health and Human
Services**
Division for Children and Youth
Services
129 Pleasant Street
Concord, NH 03301
Phone: 603-271-4707
Fax: 603-271-4729
www.nacac.org/stateprofiles/new
hamsphire.html
E-mail: catkins@dhhs.state.nh.us

NEW JERSEY
**New Jersey Department of Health
and Human Services**
Division of Children, Youth, and
Families
50 East State
Trenton, NJ 08625-0717
Phone: 609-984-2380
Fax: 609-984-5449
www.state.nj.us/umanservices/
adoption/adopt.html

NEW MEXICO
**New Mexico Children, Youth, and
Families Department**
P.O. Drawer 5160
Santa Fe, MN 87502-5160
Phone: 505-827-8456,
(toll-free) 800-432-2075
Fax: 505-827-8480
www.state.nm.us/cyfd/adopt.htm

NEW YORK
**New York State Office of Children
and Family Services**
New York State Adoption Services
52 Washington Street, Room 322
North Rensselaer, NY 12144
Phone: 518-474-9406,
Fax: 518-486-6326
www.dfa.state.ny.us/adopt/
adoption.htm

NORTH CAROLINA
**North Carolina Department
of Health and Human
Services**
Division of Social Services,
Children's Services Section
325 North Salisbury Street
2401 Mail Service Center
Raleigh, NC 27699-2411
Phone: 919-733-3801,
(toll-free) 877-NCKIDS-1
Fax: 919-715-6396
www.dhhs.state.nc.us/dss/adopt

NORTH DAKOTA
**North Dakota Department of
Human Services**
600 East Boulevard Avenue,
Dept. 325
Bismarck, ND 58505-0250
Phone: 701-328-2359
(toll-free) 800-472-2622
Fax: 701-328-2359
www.state.nd.us/humanservices

OHIO
**Ohio Department of Job and
Family Services**
Ohio Family and Children First
17 South High Street
Columbus, OH 43215
Phone: 614-466-6282
Fax: 614-466-2815
www.state.oh.us/
E-mail: webmaster@odhs.state.
oh.us

OKLAHOMA
**Oklahoma Department of Human
Services**
Division of Children and Family
Services
P.O. Box 25352
Oklahoma City, OK 73125
Phone: 405-521-2475, (toll-free)
877-657-9438
Fax: 405-521-4373
www.okdhs.org/adopt

OREGON
**Oregon Department of Human
Services**
State Office for Services to
Children and Families
Adoption Registry, 2nd Floor
South
500 Summer Street NE, E71
Salem, OR 97301-1068
Phone: 503-945-5651
Fax: 503-581-6198
www.scf.hr.state.or.us/ar

PENNSYLVANIA
**Pennsylvania Department of
Public Welfare**
Office of Children, Youth, and
Families
P.O. Box 2675
Harrisburg, PA 17105-2675
Phone: 717-787-4756 (toll-free)
800-585-SWAN
Fax: 717-705-0362
www.dpw.state.pa.us/ocyf/
ocyfas.asp

RHODE ISLAND
**Rhode Island Department for
Children, Youth, and Family
Services**
500 Prospect Street
Pawtucket, RI 02860
Phone: 401-724-1910
Fax: 401-254-7099
www.adoptionri.or
E-mail: adoptionri@ids.net

SOUTH CAROLINA
**South Carolina Department of
Social Services**
Division of Adoption and Birth
Parent Services
P.O. Box 1520
Columbia, SC 29202-1520
Phone: 803-898-7561
(toll-free) 888-CARE-4-US
Fax: 803-898-7561
www.state.sc.us/dss/adoption

SOUTH DAKOTA
**South Dakota Department of
Social Services**
Child Protection Services
700 Governor's Drive
Pierre, SD 57501-2291
Phone: 605-773-3227
Fax: 605-773-6834
www.state.sd.us/social/cps/
adoption/index.htm
E-mail: CPS@dss.state.sd.US

TENNESSEE
**Tennessee Department of
Children's Services**
436 Sixth Avenue North, Cordell
Hull Building, 7th Floor
Nashville, TN 37243-0290
Phone: 615-741-9701
Fax: 615-532-6495
www.state.tn.us/youth/adoption/

TEXAS
**Texas Department of
Protective and Regulatory
Services**
P.O. Box 149030 E-557
Austin, TX 78714-9030
Phone: 512-438-4800
Fax: 512-438-3782
www.tdprs.state.tx.us

UTAH
**Utah Department of Human
Services**
Division of Child and Family
Services

120 North 200 West, Room 225
Salt Lake City, UT 84103
Phone: 801-538-4100
Fax: 801-538-3993
www.hsdcfs.state.ut.us

VERMONT
**Vermont Department of
Social and Rehabilitation
Services**
103 South Main Street
Waterbury, VT 05671-2401
Phone: 802-241-2100
Fax: 802-241-2980
www.state.vt.us/srs/

VIRGINIA
**Virginia Department of Social
Services**
Division of Family Services
730 East Broad Street
Richmond, VA 23219
Phone: 804-692-1900
Fax: 804-692-1284
www.dss.state.va.us/

WASHINGTON
**Washington Department of
Social and Health
Services**
Division of Children and Family
Services
P.O. Box 45713
Olympia, WA 98504
Phone: 360-902-7959
Fax: 360-902-7903
www.wa.gov/dshs/

WEST VIRGINIA
West Virginia Department of Health and Human Resources
Office of Social Services
350 Capitol Street, Room 691
Charleston, WV 25301-3704
Phone: 304-558-4303
Fax: 304-558-8800
www.wvdhhr.org/oss/children/adoption.htm

WISCONSIN
Wisconsin Department of Health and Family Services
Division of Child and Family Services

P.O. Box 8916
Madison, WI 53708-8916
Phone: 608-266-3595
Fax: 608-264-6750
www.dhfs.state.wi.us/children/adoption/index.htm

WYOMING
Wyoming Department of Family Services
2300 Capitol Avenue, Hathaway Building, 3rd Floor
Cheyenne, WY 82002
Phone: 307-777-3570
Fax: 307-777-3693
www.dfsweb.state.wy.us/CHILDSVC/TOC1.HTM

ADOPTION COUNSELORS

Many different types of professionals provide counseling services. However, not all are knowledgeable and experienced about adoption. It often takes time to identify the best counselor for your particular needs. To locate a referral, contact your community adoption support group or ask your adoption professional. In addition, national professional organizations will provide you with information regarding counselors who specialize in adoption issues. Listed below are some of the different professional organization offering adoption counseling.

The American Psychological Association
750 First Street, NE
Washington, D.C. 2002
(202) 336-5510, (toll-free) 800-374-2721
www.apa.org
A clinical psychologist has completed a doctoral degree (Psy.D. or Ph.D.) in psychology and usually has completed advanced courses in child devel-

opment and psychotherapy techniques and counseling. Many clinical psychologists develop a subspecialty in child and adolescent development, family therapy and adoption, and infertility issues.

The American Psychiatric Association
1000 Wilson Boulevard, Suite 1825
Arlington, VA 22209-3901
703-907-7300
www.psych.org
E-mail: apap@psych.org

Psychiatrists are medical doctors (M.D.) who specialize in the evaluation of major mental or emotional disorders, some of which may require medication. Psychiatrists complete medical school, followed by postgraduate training in psychiatric disorders. Psychiatrists may conduct counseling themselves, or refer to other specialists in child and family therapy.

The National Association of Social Workers
750 First Street, NE
Suite 700
Washington, D.C. 2002-4241
202-408-8600
www.naswdc.org

Clinical social workers (LCSW or MSW) complete a master's degree in social work with a focus on family structure. Most address social, education, and family issues and many have met state licensure requirements to offer counseling to individuals and families.

The American Association of Marriage and Family Therapy
112 South Alfred Street
Alexandria, VA 22314-3061
(703) 838-9808
Fax: 703-838-9805

Marriage and family therapists have master's degrees (MSW) in counseling techniques with a primary focus on family and couples relationships. They typically address communication building, family structure, and boundaries within the family.

SAMPLE HOME STUDY

REFERRAL SOURCE

Anne and David Baker, or "Dave," as he prefers to be called, contacted this agency to arrange for an adoptive home study for the purpose of a domestic adoption. The Bakers were referred by their attorney, John Smith.

REQUEST AND MOTIVATION

Anne and Dave are seeking to adopt a Caucasian infant in normal health. The couple is open to a child of either sex. They have not yet connected with a prospective birth parent, but plan to place adoption advertisements in both online and regional newspapers to actively search for a successful arrangement.

Ten years ago doctors discovered a growth in Anne's uterus that was removed during a partial hysterectomy. When Anne and Dave married they were aware that they would not be able to give birth to children and were already thinking of adoption. Dave comes from a large family and has always had a fondness for children. As an elementary school teacher who loves her work with children, Anne has become aware of how much she wishes to become a mother and raise a family. This, together with the stability of the couple's situation and home life, makes the timing right for them to adopt. They have a great deal of love to share with a child.

Dave and Anne have stated that they have never been previously rejected as prospective adoptive parents, nor are they the subject of an unfavorable home study. The Bakers have been advised of the processing specifics for domestic adoption.

ADOPTIONS ISSUES

Mr. and Mrs. Baker have undertaken several activities designed to further their understanding of adoption. For example, they have read a number of books about adoption and are members of RESOLVE. They are currently attending a local support group for those interested in domestic adoption. Both applicants appear to have a good understanding of the adoption process and the unique issues involved in raising an adopted child. They seem confident about their ability to fully accept and love their adopted child. They are aware of the importance of openly communicating to their child about adoption at an appropriate age. They have a positive attitude toward birth parents and appreciate the courage required for a birth parent to place a child for adoption. They also are aware and feel secure about the possibility that their child may someday seek a meeting with her birth parents. The Bakers agree to assist their child in visiting the biological parents if she wishes, when she is of age. If they are blessed with an open adoption, they hope to stay in touch with the birth parents through letters and photos. Dave and Anne are also comfortable in communicating with prospective birth parents before a placement occurs. If they are successful, the Bakers plan to involve their child in play dates and social activities with other adopted children.

ADOPTIVE MOTHER

Anne is Caucasian, five feet six inches tall and weighs one hundred and twenty pounds. She is a vivacious, intelligent woman described by her husband as outgoing, compassionate, sensible, loving, and a "doer." She enjoys ocean sports, cycling, hiking, gardening, and reading. She does not smoke or drink.

Anne was born on July 23, 1966, in Philadelphia, Pennsylvania, but her family moved to Florida shortly after her birth. Anne's parents gave her a loving, stimulating, and supportive childhood. Currently retired to Florida and California, they continue to enjoy good health and prodigious energy.

As a child, Anne was always a good student. She went to the University of Florida, where she graduated with a degree in early education in 1979. She worked in the Palm Beach County public school system before moving to California, a place she had learned to love from previous vacations. After her move, Anne took some time off while she studied for the California licensing exam, and then resumed her work as an elementary school teacher, this time in a private educational setting. Today, she is a respected educator and advocate for children's issues in the community. If successful in their attempt to adopt, Anne plans to stop work to be a full-time mother.

ADOPTIVE FATHER

Dave is Caucasian, six feet tall and weights one hundred and seventy-five pounds. He is an active and talented sport person. As a teen, he competed in cross-country skiing. Later he took up cycling, something he and Anne now do together often. Anne describes Dave as loving, sensitive, considerate, sentimental, and especially gifted with children. Scott does not smoke and is in excellent health.

Dave was born on August 12, 1963, in Great Lakes, Illinois, a naval training center. Dave's father was in the navy for thirteen years and then left the service in San Diego and lived in the Los Angeles area awhile before moving the family to the Colorado countryside. Dave remembers growing up with horses and many opportunities for skiing, hiking, and camping. Dave is the oldest of four children. He is very close to his sister Terri, and communicates frequently with his two younger brothers, Michael and Peter.

Even at a young age, Dave was very sensitive to art. The support of his loving parents guided his natural interest to a career in art. He attended Colorado State University for a while, but did not obtain a degree. In 1971 he came to California and developed his career as an artist. Since then he has gone on to become a successful regional watercolor painter. His current joy is to teach art classes for young children in the local public school system. The fact that he is greatly loved by the kids is evidence by the many cards he has received from them. Recently, Dave has become trained as a cinema photographer and currently works on local film and movie productions. This growing business adds an additional $20,000–$30,000 per year to his other sources of income.

MARRIAGE

Dave and Anne met at a cycling event. They dated for three years before being married on August 21, 1997. They have a common passion for children, as well as a love of the country and the ocean. They are both comfortable with housework, can cook, and have the excellent, intelligent, and gentle conversations of respectful, talented people. The Bakers employ good communication techniques and compromise to resolve any difficulties that may arise. The Bakers' marriage appears based on a strong and trusting relationship.

FAMILY VALUES AND RELIGION

Anne is well educated in the development of children. She is used to working with kids and families, guiding them to more wholesome, happy lives. Dave works with kids in special and creative ways. Their experience with children has prepared them to have a family of their own. Anne and Dave are both certified in infant and child CPR and first aid and are committed to creating a safe, healthy, and stimulating environment for a child. Dave and Anne feel that family life comes first and is the biggest priority in their lives. The love and guidance they received from their own parents have set good examples for them to follow in the raising their own child. The Bakers also enjoy seeing their extended family frequently. Dave's parents live nearby and Anne's parents reside in the state part-time. Both sets of parents are eager to welcome a grandchild into the family and are extremely supportive of their children's plans to adopt.

Dave and Anne plan to take an active role in their child's moral development. The Bakers share many values in common, including the importance of family life, marriage, and contribution to their community. They have mutually set aside money to build an addition to their home, should it become necessary in the future. In addition, the Bakers have saved money for the purpose of adopting a child.

HOME AND COMMUNITY

The Bakers' home meets all the requirements of the State of California for the needs of the prospective adoptive child. Their home is close to schools, medical facilities, and community shopping, all within about fifteen minutes. Their house is situated in a rural-type estate setting. There is a remote-controlled security gate at the entrance of the property. The home is a custom-designed, spacious, two-bedroom and two-bath home. The couple has plans to add a children's wing with two more bedrooms and a bathroom, plus a family playroom.

FINANCES

Family finances were verified from the last filed income tax return. The joint family income was $100,000. Annual earnings for Dave and Anne are about $50,000 per year and $35,000 respectively. Investment income also contributes to their total annual income. The Bakers have joint cash savings of about $50,000, and investment and retirements accounts of $200,000. The family home is worth about $450,000. The Bakers have no debts, except their monthly mortgage payment of $1,050. They have medical insurance which will cover the needs of an adopted child.

HEALTH

The applicants have stated they have no history of domestic violence, substance, child, or sexual abuse, or psychological disturbance, and do not have any active, dangerous communicable diseases. They have been approved for adoption by their doctors.

CLEARANCES

The Bakers have stated they have no record or history of child abuse or sex abuse and no unrecorded offenses. They have been cleared by the California Criminal Justice Data Center and Child Protective Services.

REFERENCES AND RECOMMENDATION

Dave and Anne Baker are highly regarded by their references as persons of good character who will be excellent parents. Based upon my interviews, observations, the recommendations and documentation presented to me, it is a pleasure to recommend the Bakers for the placement of a child as young as possible of either sex.

ADOPTION ADVERTISING

ON-LINE PARENT REGISTRIES

Internet parent registries are designed to help prospective adoptive parents meet. Take the time to visit several sites before selecting a registry. The site you select should meet your individual needs as affordably as possible, while exposing your profile to many different potential birth mothers. Although many more exist, the following sites are a good sample of solid on-line registries. Many on-line parent registries exist but as the on-line landscape changes frequently, it is difficult to offer up-to-the-moment information.

Adoption.com
www.adoption.com; sister sites include Adopting.com (www.adopting.com)
and Adoption.org (www.adoption.org)

Adoptiononline.com
www.adoptiononline.com

The Link Adoption Consultants
www.linkadoption.com

Adoptionconnection.org
www.adoptionconnection.org

Adoption Network
www.adoptionnetwork.com

NEWSPAPER RESOURCES

Many different types of newspapers accept adoption advertisements, including dailies, networks, college papers, ethnic papers, and pennysavers. The number of newspapers within each category can often be quite large. Therefore, the list that follows is not comprehensive, but rather offers a sample from each of the different types. In addition, an effort has been made to list only newspapers in the states that permit adoption advertising. But the laws of some states may have changed since this list was compiled. Remember, too, that some of the newspaper contact information listed below may have been changed recently. To check the most current information, go online. Use one of the major search engines to search under keywords such as "newspaper directory," "ethnic newspapers," or "college newspapers." Newspapers can also be located in the *Gale Directory of Publications* and *The Editor and Publisher Yearbook*, found in library reference rooms.

DAILY NEWSPAPERS

News Directory
www.newsdirectory.com

News Link
www.newslink.com

Newspaper Links
www.newspaperlinks.com

NEWSPAPER NETWORKS

Alabama Press Association
3324 Independence, Suite 200, Birmingham, AL 35209
Phone: 205-871-7737; www.alabamapress.org

Alaska Newspaper Association
P.O. Box 7900
Ketchikan, AK 99901
Phone: 907-225-3157

Arizona Newspapers Association
1001 North Central
Suite 670
Phoenix, AZ 85004
Phone: 602-261-7655
www.ananews.com
E-mail: office@ananews.com

Arkansas Press Association
411 South Victory
Little Rock, AR 72201-2932
Phone: 501-374-1500
www.arkansaspress.org
E-mail: apamail@arkansaspress.org

Colorado Press Association
1336 Glenarm Place
Denver, CO 80204
Phone: 303-571-5117
www.newmedia.colorado.edu/cpa/
   online

Connecticut Daily Newspaper
Association
P.O. Box 456
West Falmouth, MA 02574
Phone: 508-548-3635

Florida Press Service
2636 Mitcham Drive
Tallahassee, FL 32308

Phone: 850-222-6401
www.flpress.com

Hoosier State Press Association
One Virginia Avenue
Suite 701
Indianapolis, IN 46204
Phone: 317-803-4772
www.haspa.com

Iowa Press Association
319 E. 5th Street
Des Moines, IA 50309
Phone: 515-244-2145
www.inanews.com

Louisiana Press Association
404 Europe Street
Baton Rouge, LA 70802
Phone: 225-344-9309
www.lapress.com

Maine Press Association
2 Old Post Road
York, ME 03909
Phone: 207-351-1033
www.mainepress.org

Michigan Press Association
827 North Washington Avenue
Lansing, MI 48906-5199
Phone: 517-372-2424
www.michiganpress.org
E-mail: mpa@michiganpress.org

Minnesota Newspaper Association
12 South 6th Street
Suite 1120
Minneapolis, MN 55402-1502
Phone: 612-332-8844
www.mnnewspapernet.org
E-mail: mna@mna.org

Mississippi Press Association
351 Edgewood Terrace
Jackson, MS 39206
Phone: 601-981-3060
www.mspress.org
E-mail: mpa@mspress.org

Missouri Press Association
802 Locust Street
Columbia, MO 65201
Phone: 573-449-4167
www.mopress.com

New Hampshire Press Association
P.O. Box 1419
Derry, NH 03038
Phone: 603-432-2048
www.nhpress.org

New Jersey Press Association
840 Bear Tavern Road
Suite 305
West Trenton, NJ 08628-1019
Phone: 609-406-0600
www.njpa.org
E-mail: njpress@njpa.org

New Mexico Press Association
2531 Wyoming Boulevard NE
Albuquerque, NM 87112
Phone: 505-275-1377
www.nmpress.org
E-mail: nmpress@earthlink.net

New York Newspaper Publishers Association
120 Washington Avenue
Albany, NY 12210
Phone: 518-449-1667
www.nynpa.com
E-mail: nynpa@nynpa.com

New York Press Association
1681 Western Avenue
Albany, NY 12203-4305
Phone: 518-464-6483
www.nynewspapers.com
E-mail: nypa@nynewspapers.com

Oklahoma Press Association
3601 North Lincoln Boulevard
Oklahoma City, OK 73105-5499
Phone: 405-524-4421
www.okpress.com

Oregon Newspaper Publishers Association
7150 SW Hampton Street, Suite 111
Portland, OR 97223
Phone: 503-624-6397
www.orenews.com
E-mail: onpa@orenews.com

**Pennsylvania Newspaper
Association**
3899 N. Front Street
Harrisburg, PA 17110
Phone: 717-703-3000
www.pa-newspaper.org
E-mail: info@pa-news.org

**South Carolina Press
Association**
PO Box 11429
Columbia, SC 29211
Phone: 803-750-9561
www.scpress.org
E-mail: scpress@scpress.org

**South Dakota Newspaper
Association**
527 Main Avenue, Suite 202
Brookings, SD 57006
Phone: 605-692-4300
www.zwire.com

Tennessee Press Association
6915 Office Park Circle
Knoxville, TN 37909
Phone: 865-584-5761
www.tntoday.com

**Texas Daily Newspaper
Association**
3101 Bee Cave Road
Suite 250
Austin, TX 78746-5574
Phone: 512-476-4351
www.tdna.org
E-mail: info@tdna.org

Utah Press Association
307 W 200, Suite 4006
Salt Lake City, UT 84101
Phone: 801-328-8678
www.utahpress.com

Vermont Press Association
One Winooski Park
Colchester, VT 05439
Phone: 802-654-2442

Virginia Press Association
11529 Nuckols Road
Glen Allen, VA 23059
Phone: 804-521-7570
www.vpa.net

**Washington Newspaper Publishers
Association**
3838 Stone Way North
Seattle, WA 98103
Phone: 206-634-3837
www.wnpa.com

West Virginia Press Association
3422 Pennsylvania Avenue
Charleston, WV 25302
Phone: 304-342-1011
www.wvpress.org
E-mail: wvpress@earthlink.net

Wyoming Press Association
2121 Evans Avenue
Cheyenne, WY 82001
Phone: 307-635-3905
www.wyopress.org
E-mail: wypress@trib.com

ETHNIC NEWSPAPERS

Many ethnic newspapers are distributed around the country. The newspapers listed below are a sample. For a more thorough listing, go on-line and search under the keywords "ethnic newspapers."

Arizona Jewish Post
2601 North Campbell Ave.
Suite 205
Tucson, AZ 85719
Phone: 520-319-1112
www.jewishtucson.org

Deep South Jewish Voice
P.O. Box 130052
Birmingham, AL 35213
Phone: 205-595-9255
www.deepsouthjewishvoice.com/
E-mail: information@deepsouth
    jewishvoice.com

The Irish Echo
309 Fifth Avenue
New York, NY 10016-6548
Phone: 212-686-1266
Toll-free: 888-447-4743
www.irishisk.com/html/body_iep.
    html

The Irish Voice
432 Park Avenue South

Suite 1503
New York, NY 10016
Phone: 212-684-3366
www.irishvoice.com
E-mail: IRVCE@aol.com

The Irish Edition
903 East Willow Grove Ave.
Wyndmoor, PA 19038-7909
Phone: 215-836-4900
www.irishedition.net
E-mail: IRED@voicenet.com

Washington Afro-American Tribune
1612 14th Street, NW
Washington, DC 20009
Phone: 202-332-0080

Black Focus Newsweekly
2021 East 52nd Street
Suite 211
Indianapolis, IN 46205
www.blackfocus.com
E-mail: blackfocus@hotmail.com

PENNYSAVERS AND SHOPPERS

Thousands of pennysavers and shoppers are distributed locally and regionally in this country. Many are affiliated with sister papers. For a more complete list of current papers, search on-line under *pennysavers*.

Thrifty Nickel Want Ads
500 42nd Avenue
East Moline, IL 61244
Phone: 309-792-4747
The largest free want ad paper in
the United States. Offers national
and regional advertising.

Volusia Pennysaver
245 South Woodland Blvd.
DeLand, FL 32720
Phone: 386-736-2880
www.floridapennysavers.com
With its sister papers, serves North-
east and Central Florida.

**Turnpikes and Hall of Fame
Pennysavers**
P.O. Box 671
64 Lake Street
Richfield Springs, NY 13439
Phone: 315-858-1730
www.pennysaveronline.com
Reaches six counties in New York

Tucson Shopper
1861 West Grant Road
Tucson, AZ 85745
Phone: 502-622-0101
www.members.aol.com/shopperads

COLLEGE NEWSPAPERS

There are over a thousand college newspapers across the country. To find
the most current contact information about campus papers, go on-line.
Many Internet sites offer college paper directories.

News Directory
www.newsdirectory.com

Ecola
www.ecola.com

College News
www.collegenews.com

INTERNET SEARCH ENGINES

Although there are many search engines currently on the Web, only a few
are well-known or well-used. Because these major search engines can
potentially generate so much traffic, they are the most important places to
be listed. In the past, payment was not required to add a site to an
engine's database. Today, most major search engines charge to be listed
within a reasonable time. Also, some search engines do not have their own

database. Instead they use other directories and search engines to supply data.

Some of the major search engines are listed below. Because this information changes frequently, consult one of the search engine news sites for the most current listings. One good site is Search Engine Watch (www.searchenginewatch.com). Here you will find extensive information on all aspects of search engines, including the top search engines, submission requirements, and tips on completing the registration process, improving placement, and searching the Web more effectively.

Google
A highly recommended site. Submissions are currently free.

Yahoo
Launched in 1994, Yahoo is the Web's oldest directory. Personal site submissions are currently free.

MSN Search
Considered a good search engine with many valuable features. Relies in part on other search providers, such as LookSmart. Those seeking submission must be listed with search providers LookSmart and Inktomi.

AOL Search
AOL Search provides users with listings that come from Google's index. Those seeking membership must be listed with Google.

Open Directory
The Open Directory was formerly known as NewHoo and was acquired by AOL Time Warner in 1998. Submissions are currently free.

Alta Vista
Alta Vista, launched in 1995, is one of the oldest search engines on the Web. Submissions are currently free.

Selected References

Numerous books are available covering many different aspects of adoption, including open adoption, domestic adoption, international adoption, special-needs adoption, and adoptive parent issues. The following list is not comprehensive, but rather offers a sample of some good books. As you progress with your own research, you may discover many other books that will assist you. The books below are currently available in libaries and bookstores.

Adamec, Chris (1998). *The Complete Idiot's Guide to Adoption*. New York: Alpha Books.

Barth, R. P., and Berry, M. (1988). *Adoption and Disruption: Rates, Risks, and Responses*. Hawthorne, NY: Adline de Gruyter.

Beauvais-Godwin, Laura, and Godwin, Raymond (2000). *The Complete Adoption Book: Everything You Need to Know to Adopt a Child* (2nd ed.). Holbrook, MA: Adams Media.

Gilman, Lois (1998). *The Adoption Resource Book* (4th ed.). New York: HarperCollins.

Handel, Nelson (2001). *Reaching Out: The Guide to Writing a Terrific Dear Birthmother Letter* (1st electronic ed. on-line) Los Angeles: EasternEdge Press.

Hicks, Randall B. (1999). *Adopting in America: How to Adopt Within One Year* (2nd ed.). Sun City, CA: WordSlinger Press.

Johnston, Patricia I. (1992). *Adopting after Infertility*. Indianapolis: Perspectives Press.

————. (1997). *Launching a Baby's Adoption: Practical Strategies for Parents and Professionals*. Indianapolis: Perspectives Press.

Marshner, Connaught, and Pierce, William (Eds.). *Adoption Factbook III*. Waite Park, MN: Park Press.

Martin, Cynthia D., and Groves, Dru M. (1998). *Beating the Adoption Odds: Using Your Head and Your Heart to Adopt* (Rev. ed.). New York: Harcourt.

McDermott, Mark T. (1993). Agency versus independent adoption: the case for independent adoption. *The Future of Children, Adoption, 3,* 146–152.

Melina, Lois R., and Roszia, Sharon K. (1993). *The Open Adoption Experience*. New York: HarperCollins.

National Endowment for Financial Education (1997). *How to Make Adoption an Affordable Option*.

National Endowment for Financial Education (1999). *Planning to Afford Family Building*.

Varon, Lee (2000). *Adoption on Your Own: The Complete Guide to Adopting as a Single Parent*. New York: Farrar, Straus and Giroux.

Wolff, Jana (2000). *Secret Thoughts of an Adoptive Mother* (2nd ed., rev.). Honolulu: Vista Communications.

INDEX

sugar, 201
surrogate mothers, trend in, 31

taxation, financial assistance, 70–72
telephone calls. *See* phone calls
timing
    commitment, birth mother/adopting
        mother relationship, 195–197
    newspaper advertising, 146–147
tradition, advertising, 134
travel
    adoption plan, 204–205
    readiness assessment, 39

uncertainty, management of, readiness
        assessment, 36–37

U.S. Census Bureau, 127
U.S. Department of Health and
    Human Services, 11

values, personal interviews, home study,
    105
visitation, contact guidelines, birth
    mother/adopting mother
    relationship, 193–194

wait. *See* delays
Web sites. *See also* Internet
    advertising content,
        153–158
    advertising costs, 139
Wolff, Jana, 33